The Lord of Bellavista

The Lord of Bellavista

DAVID MILLER

TRIANGLE

First published in Great Britain in 1998 by
Triangle,
SPCK,
Marylebone Road,
London NW1 4DU

Third impression 1999.

Scripture quotations are from
The Revised Standard Version of the Bible © 1971 and 1952.

British Library Cataloguing-in-Publication Data
A catalogue record for this book is available
from the British Library

ISBN 0–281–05128–3

Photoset by Pioneer Associates, Perthshire
Printed in Great Britain by
Caledonian International, Glasgow

To Barbara, of course

Contents

List of Characters

Amador, José. Inmate in Picaleña Penitentiary, Ibagué.

Archila, Francisco. Prison Fellowship volunteer in Medellín.

Arroyave, Fernando. Embittered police officer turned *sicario*. Accepted Christ in 1991 in Bellavista. Later transferred to Picaleña Penitentiary in Ibagué.

Bonilla, Fernando. Governor of Bellavista Jail when Oscar Osorio began his chaplain ministry.

Brabon, David, MD. Bogotá surgeon and brother of Jeannine Brabon. Married to Patricia Martinez.

Brabon, Jeannine. OMS missionary. Professor of Old Testament at the Biblical Seminary of Colombia and founding member of Prison Fellowship of Antioquia.

Carvajal, Cardona (Dr). Governor of La Ladera prison who first invited Donald and Georgia Rendle to work there.

Casteñeda, Manuel. Prison evangelist who met Oscar Osorio at a street meeting and introduced him to Bellavista Jail.

Castro, Martha. Career employee of Colombia Justice Ministry. Introduced Jeannine Brabon to Gustavo De Greiff.

Celis, Javier and Victor. Missionaries of the Covenant Evangelical Church. Prison Fellowship volunteers in Medellín.

Chalarca, Jairo. Pastor of the Covenant Evangelical Church in Villa Hermosa. Brought Oscar Osorio to Christ. Later preached in the white flag evangelistic campaign inside Bellavista.

Claros, José. Inmate in Picaleña Penitentiary, Ibagué.

Colorado, Adán. Bellavista inmate. Accepted Christ in 1986.

Following his release, he founded the Rehoboth Jireh Centre for substance abusers.

Colson, Charles. Member of White House staff during Richard Nixon's administration. Founder of Prison Fellowship.

Correa, Mary Luz. Graduate of the Biblical Seminary of Colombia. Full-time staff member of Prison Fellowship of Antioquia.

Correa, Victor. University student imprisoned in Bellavista for ties to urban guerrillas. Accepted Christ through the influence of José Giraldo.

Cortez, Fabian. Graduate of the Biblical Seminary of Colombia. First academic dean of the Bellavista Bible Institute.

De Greiff, Gustavo (Dr). First Prosecutor General of Colombia. Headed the investigation that culminated in the apprehension of Pablo Escobar. Later appointed ambassador to Mexico.

Donado, Luz Dary. Widow of Walter Donado, who was murdered by a youth gang in Medellín in 1997.

Donner, Theo. Vice-rector of the Biblical Seminary of Colombia.

Escobar, Pablo. Multi-millionaire founder and kingpin of the Medellín drug cartel. Killed in a gunfight with anti-narcotics police in December 1993.

Espinoza, Renzo. Student at the Biblical Seminary of Colombia. Taught classes at the Bellavista Bible Institute in 1992.

Giraldo, José. Arrested in 1990 for kidnapping. Accepted Christ in Bellavista and taught classes in the prison's P3 centre. Married to Luz Dary Ocampo.

Giraldo, Román. Imprisoned in Bellavista in July 1991 for theft. Accepted Christ and later joined the staff of Prison Fellowship of Antioquia.

Gonzalez, Jorge Luis. Imprisoned on terrorism charges. Accepted Christ in Bellavista in July 1994 while studying under José Giraldo in the P3 centre.

Henao, Jan Mario (alias). *Sicario* employed by the Medellín drug cartel and friend of Juan Carlos Londoño. Accepted Christ in Bellavista. Married Liliana on 4 October, 1996, in the Prison Chapel.

Henao, Margarita. Student at the Biblical Seminary of Colombia who searched the city morgues with Jeannine Brabon for the body of her brother, Gustavo.

Hernandez, Lacides. Graduate of the Biblical Seminary of Colombia. Full-time staff member of Prison Fellowship of Antioquia.

Herrera, Ariel 'Charli'. Inmate in Picaleña Penitentiary, Ibagué.

Ibarra, Nelson. Nephew of 'Papa' Gerardo Pino. Accepted Christ in 1996 at the New Life Post Penal Centre through the influence of his uncle.

Lewis, Gwyn. Missionary of the Covenant Evangelical Church and Prison Fellowship volunteer in Medellín.

Londoño, Juan, alias 'Juan Caca'. Specialized in building car bombs for the Medellín drug cartel. Accepted Christ in 1993 in Bogotá prison. Married Gloria on 4 October, 1996, in the Bellavista Prison Chapel.

Lopez, Imelda (Dr). Governor of Picaleña Penitentiary when Fangio Quiroz began his chaplain ministry there.

Lopez, Orlando (Dr). Vice-governor of Bellavista. Employed by INPEC since 1989.

Madrid Malo, Mario (Dr). Bogotá Attorney. Director of Guillermo Cano Institute on Human Rights.

Maestre, Nehemias. Christian inmate in La Ladera who prayed for God to send evangelists.

Mazo, Mario. First pastor of Bellavista chapel.

Morales, Horacio. Inmate who first witnessed to Adán Colorado. Later joined him in opening the Rehoboth Jireh Centre for substance abusers.

Mosquera, Jaiber. Imprisoned in Bellavista in 1986 for car theft. Wounded in prison riots in 1990. Accepted Christ at the New Life Post Penal Centre following his release.

Muñoz, 'Mama' Lilian de. Prison Fellowship volunteer in Medellín.

Murillo, Daniel. Teenage *sicario* and gang leader. Accepted Christ in Bellavista in 1994 through the influence of Oscar Osorio.

Osorio, Carmenza (Perez). Wife of Oscar Osorio.

Osorio, Ernesto and Genoveva. Oscar Osorio's parents.

Osorio, Oscar. Former drug dealer and thief. Chaplain in Bellavista Jail since 1987. In 1992, became full-time staff member of Prison Fellowship of Antioquia.

Paez, Gilberto (alias). Medellín *sicario* employed by the Medellín drug cartel and imprisoned for homicide. Accepted Christ in Bellavista through influence of José Giraldo.

Palacios, Nelson. Former *sicario*. Prison Fellowship worker who accompanied Jorge Luis Gonzalez on his ill-fated visit to Valencia in 1996.

Perez, Mery. Mother of Carmenza Perez Osorio.

Pino, Gerardo 'Papa'. Imprisoned 18 times for armed robbery, was converted in Bellavista in March 1988.

Quiroz, Fangio. Distant relative of Pablo Escobar who accepted Christ at the Central Pan American Church of Medellín. Later joined Prison Fellowship staff and was assigned to Picaleña Penitentiary in Ibagué. Married to Doris Gomez.

Ramirez, Hader. Governor of Bellavista Jail in 1990. Gave Oscar Osorio permission to conduct the white flag evangelistic campaign.

Rendle, Donald and Georgia. Canadian missionary couple who initiated prison ministry in La Ladera in 1975. In 1982 founded Prison Fellowship of Colombia.

Rodriguez, Maria. Single mother of 14 who began prison ministry in 1967 in Ibagué.

Rojas, Manuel. Prison Fellowship volunteer in Medellín.

Socha Salamanca, Gustavo (Colonel). National Director General of Prisons in Colombia in 1992, when Bellavista Bible Institute was organized.

Taborda, Orlando. Professional *sicario* who accepted Christ in Bellavista in early 1990. Participated in the white flag evangelistic campaign. Later transferred to Calarca prison.

Taborda, Oscar. Bellavista inmate murdered by fellow prisoners for allegedly informing on the drug cartel.

Torres, Luz Elena. Director of the Penitentiary Pedagogical Programme, 'P3', in Bellavista Jail.

Voelkel, Jack and Mary Ann. Professors at the Biblical Seminary of Colombia.

Wittig, Mark. OMS missionary. Professor at the Biblical Seminary of Colombia and founder of youth sports clubs.

1

The Walls

A skull and crossbones painted on the prison wall greeted Oscar Osorio as he turned the corner. He was on his way from the governor's office to Cell Block Eight and there he saw it, ugly, rust red, painted with congealed blood. The mutilated corpse of a prisoner lay nearby, flies buzzing about the oozing knife wounds.

Oscar drew a breath and walked on. He had seen dozens of corpses in the corridors of Bellavista during his years as a volunteer prison minister. One could not help encountering dead bodies in this concrete hell. On average, Bellavista prisoners murdered two of their fellow inmates every day. Wars between rival cell blocks dramatically increased the body-count. On those days, the dead lay in the corridors for hours before wary guards collected them for burial.

The thing that shocked Oscar these days was the gruesome graffiti the killers had taken to splashing on prison walls. As he walked along the perimeter of a cell block, he saw crimson sketches of corpses, guns, knives. The cement above one victim carried an obscene epitaph, scrawled with the dead man's own blood. The grisly artwork was intended to advertise the assassin's flair for brutality and show contempt for his victim. It worked.

In 1990, Bellavista prison was exploding with violence. Pablo Escobar, the cocaine king of Colombia and strong man of the Medellín drug cartel, had declared war on law enforcement. Cartel operatives were systematically murdering guards. Escobar had ordered his soldiers in the jail to offer correctional officers a choice. They could make extra money by cooperating with the cartel to smuggle weapons into Bellavista and aid prisoners to escape, or they could die for refusing to help. Corruption paid well. Integrity got you killed.

Oscar Osorio witnessed the high-stakes death game turn into unchecked blood-lust. Days before, he had witnessed drive-by gunmen murder an officer of the guard while the man waited for a taxi at the prison gate. Unsuspecting guards were being killed on buses, while waiting in cars at traffic lights, even in their own living rooms with their families looking on.

The carnage reached such proportions that Bellavista's security staff refused to enter the prison. They went on strike, allowing no one inside, not even the governor himself. Meanwhile, officers distributed leaflets outside the main gate to passers-by as part of a campaign to sensitize the public to their plight. They described the horrors inside Bellavista and appealed for the army to storm the prison and crush the rebellion.

A demonic, mob mentality had seized the inmates inside the jail. They turned on one another in mindless aggression, as if under the spell of some dark lord of death. In all his years in Bellavista, Oscar had never seen savage killings like these. Murderers hacked their victims with 100, 200 knife wounds. They cut off heads, gouged out eyes, cut off arms and legs.

Osorio reached Cell Block Eight, where he had arranged to meet with a group of Christian believers. He stopped in the patio to watch two teams of inmates playing a game of football. Their sport presented a bizarre contrast to the rioting around them. Oscar looked more closely and saw that, in fact, what they were kicking around was a human head.

A spasm of nausea gripped the preacher. He reeled back and blurted out an urgent prayer. 'Lord, where have you brought me? I left a life of crime to preach the gospel, and you call me here!'

Medellín, 1967

Oscar Osorio launched his criminal career as a boy in a small grocery shop in Villa Hermosa, the Medellín borough where he lived. He chose the shop carefully. An elderly woman owned it and conducted business in the traditional Colombian way. Oscar had watched her fill orders, choosing each item individually from the shelves on the back wall and placing them on the high counter that separated her and her merchandise from the customers. Once in a while, she used a movable ladder to reach the tins on the higher shelves.

Oscar placed his own order: rice, beans, lentils and *panela*, thick sugar cane molasses for brewing a traditional Colombian hot drink. The elderly woman wrapped the items on the counter and tallied up the price. Oscar remembered one more item he needed, a tin up on the highest shelf in the far corner of the back wall. The owner obliged and slowly ascended her ladder. When she reached the last rung, Oscar grabbed the bundle of groceries off the counter, dashed out the front door and down the street, heading for home.

Home for Oscar was a one-room brick building at the back of a dirt lot that he shared with his father, Ernesto, his mother, Genoveva, two sisters and 14 brothers.

Genoveva had not seen Ernesto for days and therefore had no money to buy food. That morning Oscar, the eighth-born of her 17 children, had gone out with a tin pail to beg table scraps from the neighbours, as he had done many times before. When he returned with his bundle of store-bought groceries, Genoveva demanded to know where he got them.

'A lady in the shop gave me these things,' Oscar lied. 'Wasn't that kind of her?'

No one had ever before given a parcel of groceries to the Osorio family. Genoveva peered sharply into her son's large brown eyes, looking for a trace of deception. He returned her steady gaze.

'Very well,' she said wearily. 'Let's get the fire going. Your brothers and sisters are hungry.'

Hunger was something the Osorio children lived with every day. Their father, a sweet-maker by trade, had moved the family to the city from his native village of Sonson, high in the Andean mountains south-east of Medellín, in order to escape a cold climate and rural poverty.

Medellín, the City of Eternal Spring, offered better weather but no escape from poverty. The Osorio children wore patches on their faded clothing and no shoes on their feet. They never slept in a bed. At night, the entire family lay down side by side on burlap sacks on the hard floor of their one-room house.

Their neighbours in Villa Hermosa labelled the Osorio family the *bonboneros* because of their peculiar trade. The mornings that Ernesto was at home, he bought sugar, corn starch and flavourings to make sweets. The older children helped prepare the confections and wrap them in brown paper. Each afternoon, Ernesto and two or three of his sons made the rounds of local shops, peddling the day's wares. When they had sold all they could, which usually occupied them until 10 or 11 o'clock at night, they spent their profits on a parcel of potatoes, rice, plantains and manioc.

The sight of Ernesto coming home with a bulging burlap sack on his shoulder always comforted Genoveva. It meant she could provide the one hot meal her family would eat that day. She and the children cooked it as soon as Ernesto arrived. Often, 'lunch' at the Osorio house was served at midnight.

Some days, Ernesto left home alone to sell his sweets, and Genoveva worried that she would not be able to provide a midnight meal for her children. If business were bad, Ernesto might get depressed and drink up what profit he made in rum or *aguardiente*. If business were good, he might feel lucky and gamble his profit away at cards or dice. Either way, Genoveva and the children would see neither Ernesto nor a hot meal for days.

On those days, Oscar and his siblings subsisted on bread and hot *panela* water. One serving, per child, per day. The diet kept them alive but did not keep the hunger away. Nor did it provide sufficient nutrients for Genoveva, who was continually pregnant, to bear healthy babies, or for the Osorio children to grow to their full stature once she had brought them into the world. Hunger as much as heredity produced the compact physique that earned Oscar a lifelong nickname, 'midget'.

*   *   *

Hunger motivated Oscar to launch his criminal career. His successful grocery shop theft encouraged him to hit juicier targets – butchers' shops, to be exact. The Osorios could seldom afford the luxury of meat, even when the sweets sold well and Ernesto avoided drink and gambling. Oscar studied butchers' shops all over Medellín, especially those far from Villa Hermosa where the chances were nil of someone recognizing him. His tactic never varied: enter the shop with shopping bag in hand like a paying customer, wait until the butcher turns his back, grab the nearest chunk of beef and dash out of the door.

The police sometimes gave chase but never caught Oscar. He might have been small for his age, but he was quick on his feet and nimble in city traffic.

'Where did you get that meat?' Genoveva would ask her son when he arrived home with his prize. 'Did you steal again?'

Oscar knew he had no hope of convincing his mother that some nice lady had given it to him, so he developed a clever argument. 'Mother, do you want us to die of hunger? Look, the rich have enough to eat, so it's no sin to rob from them, is it?'

Genoveva had little will and less energy to argue with her son. Instead she would accept the pilfered meat, start a fire going and cook the one hot meal her family would eat that day.

Had she known how well Oscar was learning to steal from the rich, Genoveva would have argued with her son about the sin of it. Along with other teenagers in the borough, Oscar was working his way up from shoplifting to assault and robbery. The youths worked in pairs, picking on women, drunks and the elderly. Once they spotted a victim on the street, they split up and approached from opposite directions. One thief grabbed the person from behind, pinning down the arms and muzzling the mouth. The other rifled through pockets and handbags and extracted money. He sometimes stripped watches off wrists or jewellery off throats. Sometimes he pulled off shoes. The operation lasted mere seconds. The hapless victim barely had time to scream for help before the thieves dashed off, dodging nimbly through city traffic.

Before he was old enough to own a driving licence, Oscar was committing armed robberies. Only one turned fatal, although Oscar himself did not do the killing. They entered a clothes shop in the city centre. His partner put a knife to the throat of the elderly man who waited on them. He told the man not to scream, that they were only going to tie him up and put him in the toilet while they helped themselves to a few pairs of blue jeans. But the old man did scream, the knife slashed his throat and blood spurted. The boys dashed out with the jeans before the police could catch them. Next day they read in the newspaper that the elderly man had died.

One robbery nearly turned fatal for Oscar himself. He and a partner named Luis targeted a greengrocer in the produce market who appeared to carry plenty of cash. It was a standard theft. Luis grabbed the fellow from behind while Oscar retrieved wads of notes from his apron pockets. The man proved stronger than their usual victims, however, and threw Luis to the ground. Oscar managed to flee before the greengrocer could tackle him.

Once safely out of jeopardy, Oscar counted the notes. They totalled 20,000 pesos, much more than the two thieves had calculated. Oscar toyed with the idea of keeping the whole lot for himself, forming a clever argument in his head. After all, Luis probably had been arrested and would not show up at the rendezvous point to divide the money. Worse yet, he probably had confessed to police, who would be waiting to arrest Oscar when he showed up at the rendezvous point. Oscar knew places in Medellín to lose himself, places where even Luis would never find him, just in case he had managed to evade the police. In the end, Oscar convinced himself to keep all the money.

He lost himself on Medellín streets for a year before going home again to Villa Hermosa. He was confident that, by then, Luis had forgotten his treachery. He was wrong. One day he stood on the pavement in front of the Osorio house smoking a marijuana cigarette when someone grabbed him from behind. Out of the corner of his eye he saw the knife coming at his chest. Oscar got his right hand up in time to deflect the blow.

The blade passed through a finger and penetrated the pectoral muscle, but did not reach his heart or lungs. The next blow struck from behind. The knife drove into the shoulder blade and lodged there. His assailant ran away, leaving the weapon dangling from Oscar's back.

The Osorios rushed Oscar to a clinic where doctors staunched his internal bleeding and stitched up his wounds. With time and physiotherapy, he regained the use of his right arm, which was nearly paralysed in the attack. He was lucky. Much luckier than the elderly man who died for a few pairs of blue jeans.

*   *   *

Colombian marijuana was dirt cheap when Oscar and his friends entered adolescence, but still out of reach for boys from poor families. So they learned to improvise their substance abuse.

They rolled their first 'joints' with ground aspirin mixed with pine cone and spider's web. The simple witch's brew produced a smoke noxious enough to knock them into a stupor for hours. A common mushroom that grew in cow manure was even more potent. The boys masked its bitter taste by covering the fungus with sugar or caramelized milk and ate it raw. The mushroom would send Oscar on a three-day sleep-walk, oblivious to home, parents or problems.

The most lethal home-made high came from *cacao sabanero*, a substance more affluent drug users assiduously avoided. It was known locally as Satan's drug, having caused irreversible brain damage in several consumers. The weed grew in thickets on the slopes above Medellín, and the boys from Villa Hermosa could harvest as many of its white, pithy seed-pods as they dared. Chewing one strong *cacao sabanero* pod would send the boys into a drugged coma lasting up to seven days. During these binges, Oscar never saw home. He slept on a sheet of cardboard in the thicket or on the street. Upon awaking, he would not know what day of the week it was and could barely remember his own name and address.

Conventional wisdom had it that chewing ten *cacao*

sabaneros would kill you. An acquaintance of Oscar's, 'El Garrote' by name, decided to test this thesis one day and was rendered permanently and irreversibly mad. Today a middle-aged El Garrote still sleeps on cardboard sheets on the streets of Medellín, when not otherwise confined to a psychiatric ward.

Thieving eventually generated enough income for Oscar and friends to afford real marijuana. They smoked it in the thickets above their homes, washing down its anaesthetic vapours with cocktails of rubbing alcohol and water. Now they could also afford Benzedrine, phenobarbitone and all manner of pills to alter consciousness. Years before it became the drug of choice in Europe and the United States, cocaine circulated among the poor boys of Villa Hermosa. The uncut powder was so pure and potent, their noses bled from inhaling it. But inhale they did, with relish. They found that cocaine instantly erased fatigue, depression and, most importantly, hunger.

Years later, someone asked Oscar if he used the dangerous drugs because he was hungry. 'No, not at all,' he replied frankly. 'It was because I hated my life. You suffered so much, you had no love for living. I was ready to die – from drugs or any other way I could find.'

*   *   *

Drugs did not send Oscar to his grave, but they did send him to jail. Soon after he started smoking marijuana, he began peddling it to other adolescents. In 1974 in Medellín, a marijuana joint sold for a mere half peso. Street dealers made only 25 *centavos* profit on each cigarette. The only people interested in selling the stuff, especially in the light of the high risks inherent in the business, were boys from poor families. Boys like Oscar Osorio.

Oscar proved a successful businessman. He discovered a large market for his merchandise at a university near his home. Most days he sold 800 cigarettes; on good days, 1,000. With that kind of volume, the 25 *centavos* profit added up to real money. Enough for him to bring home parcels of groceries and chunks of beef without having to pilfer them.

His older brothers had left home to steal and deal, but

Oscar still resided at his parents' one-room house and shared his income from drugs with the family. Ernesto and Genoveva expressed little appreciation for his generosity, however, perhaps because his presence at home regularly brought the police around to search for drugs or question Oscar about some recent hold-up. They were likewise embarrassed each time a neighbour came to inform them that their son had been found unconscious on a back street, sleeping off another drug binge. The Osorios might have been poor, but they had their pride. They let Oscar know that they considered him the black sheep of the family, who was sure to drive his mother to an early grave.

One morning Oscar was selling marijuana to a college student when the customer pulled out a gun, pointed it at Oscar's forehead and told him he was under arrest. The customer was in fact an undercover police officer who had caught Oscar with his entire stash of 1,000 incriminating cigarettes. The court sent Oscar to La Ladera prison.

Oscar found living conditions inside La Ladera, apart from the confinement, similar to what he had known most of his life. He slept on a sheet of cardboard on a cement floor, side by side with 300 other inmates who shared the same huge cell. The diet consisted of a bit of meat, lots of rice and a few vegetables, exactly what he ate at home. He did notice one difference. Here, the meat was rotten, the rice dirty and the vegetables gave him diarrhoea. As he did on the street, Oscar passed his days smoking marijuana.

Fights broke out frequently, so Oscar maintained his skill with a knife. The duels generally involved hand-to-hand combat that lasted until one inmate was dead or both were too cut up to continue. Inmates fought over simple things like T-shirts, shoes, food parcels from outside, and not-so-simple things like rape.

La Ladera did not allow conjugal visits, a policy everybody believed caused the high incidence of homosexual behaviour. Veteran prisoners accosted every new inmate, especially if he were young and comely. If a youth yielded to violation, he became a 'lady'. If he did not care to become a lady, he fought.

Oscar Osorio, still a teenager when first incarcerated in La Ladera, fought the rapists. They bloodied his face and scarred his body, but received blows and scars in kind from the determined young man. And no one in La Ladera ever succeeded in turning Oscar into a lady.

Following his first arrest, Oscar spent only 30 days in the prison before being released. Prison space in Medellín was in short supply, and the authorities had to incarcerate criminals much more dangerous than a teenage dealer of marijuana cigarettes. Oscar was back on the street for exactly six months. Then he was in jail again, this time in Sonson. The court had sentenced him to two years for armed robbery.

Oscar served the time, was released and was recaptured one month later for committing another felony. When he learned that his son was committing crimes in his native Sonson, Ernesto Osorio travelled to the small town high in the Andes to plead for clemency. The mayor offered a kind of plea bargain. Oscar would sign a notarized statement promising never again to set foot in Sonson and be released to the custody of his father. Should Oscar ever break his promise, the mayor would automatically put him back in jail for exactly 15 years.

Back in Villa Hermosa, Oscar, now 22, continued smoking dope and committing robberies. He found a girlfriend with whom he could smoke dope and commit robberies. She was Estela, 16, also of Villa Hermosa. Oscar became Estela's mentor, teaching her to pick pockets on crowded buses and snatch handbags on busy streets. He taught her how to consume every drug in his repertoire, except the deadly *cacao sabanero*, of course. He had feelings for the girl. Estela taught herself prostitution.

One day Oscar came to Estela with a proposal. How about moving to the Caribbean coast? He had learned that old enemies were looking for him to collect outstanding debts and that the police wanted him for questioning about a recent hold-up. He had always wanted to live in the tropics and thought this was a good time. Would Estela care to come?

She did. For the next five years, the couple lived together in

Barranquilla, Santa Marta and Cartagena. Mornings found them awaking in some cheap hotel before Oscar left to steal and deal and Estela to sell her body. Evenings usually saw them sitting in some dingy tavern, counting their day's income. Any money not needed for meals and lodgings went to buy marijuana, pills, rum and *aguardiente*, which they consumed together before retiring for the night in another cheap hotel.

The pair eventually drifted apart, and Oscar, confident that he had long been forgotten by the police and his old enemies, drifted back to Medellín. Unfortunately, he made new enemies. One night in a tavern he shoved a broken bottle into the face of one, and the police arrested him for attempted murder. He found himself back in jail again, this time in a prison that had been built to replace the run-down La Ladera. It was bigger, more modern, more crowded and more dangerous. Its name was Bellavista.

Medellín, Today

Assault, robbery and drug-trafficking are serious crime problems in Medellín, but they are not the city's most serious crime problem. Homicide is. In the last 40 years, textile manufacturing has transformed Medellín from a sleepy, provincial capital of 80,000 into a megalopolis of 3.2 million. However, textile manufacturing is no longer the city's most lucrative industry. Murder is. Medellín has achieved the unenviable rank of the most violent city in Colombia, the most violent country in the Americas.

Military intelligence estimates that three thousand *sicarios* – contract criminals specializing in homicide, kidnap and extortion – prowl the streets of the city. That works out to one professional killer for every one thousand residents. One hundred and twenty gangs engage in homicide for pay. Many of them are bands of neighbourhood toughs that go by designations like 'Los Magníficos', 'Los Monjes' or 'Escorpiones'. In some cases, they take charge of neighbourhood security, punishing thieves and vandals and extorting protection money for the service. In other cases, they themselves are the local thieves and vandals and terrorize all who oppose them.

The average Medellín *sicario* is 16 years of age, comes from a poor family and entertains little hope of achieving an education or landing a decent job. Murder-for-money seems his best option to escape the slum. But a low local wage scale coupled with fierce competition for contracts drives down the price for his services. This is especially true in the north-east quarter of the city, where slums have crept up the steep mountainsides. Here land is cheap and human life cheaper. Medellín *sicarios* will accept as little as US$30 to take a life.

Most ambitious young killers dream of making big bucks working for an organization at the higher end of the homicide market. *Sicarios* in this professional stratum maintain offices in the city centre, often disguised as exchange houses or accounting firms. They accept only the most lucrative contracts, mainly from politicians, wealthy businessmen and underworld bosses who can afford to pay hefty fees. Important jobs earn *sicarios* tens of thousands of dollars. When business is slow, they turn to kidnapping and extortion to bolster income. These freelance operations usually target politicians, wealthy businessmen and underworld bosses who can afford to pay hefty ransoms.

As with any business, the greater the risk, the higher the compensation. Public personalities employ cadres of bodyguards to protect them from the *sicarios*, who in turn invest in more manpower and greater firepower to carry out assignments. *Sicario* firms employ skilled investigators to stalk their prey, attractive prostitutes to lure unsuspecting victims into traps, and expert drivers to chauffeur getaway cars. Their arsenals feature the latest in automatic weapons, high-yield explosives and electronic detonators.

The brutal reality of the *sicario* industry is that few of the youths who aspire to the riches it offers live long enough to escape the poverty it breeds. Life expectancy for *sicarios* is somewhere between six months and one year. Police records show that seven out of every ten murder victims in Medellín are young men between the ages of 14 and 20. The city's *sicarios*, it appears, more frequently kill one another for free than they dispatch their victims for pay.

Intramural violence between *sicario* gangs, in fact, accounts for most deaths in the slums of Medellín. Once a youngster joins a gang, he must quickly build a reputation as a ruthless killer if he is to succeed as a *sicario*. His chances of surviving are slim, given the keen competition. It is more likely that, by becoming a paid killer, he has doomed himself to a life nasty, brutish and short.

*   *   *

On the edge of Medellín sits Bellavista National Jail. Built in 1976 to accommodate 1,500 inmates, Bellavista today holds nearly 5,000, most of them young *sicarios* and terrorists serving time for murder, kidnap or extortion. The prison is under-staffed as well as overcrowded. The 300 guards assigned to maintain security can do little more than stand sentry duty at iron gates leading to the cell blocks. Inside the cell blocks, prisoners are quartered in labyrinths of tiny plywood and cardboard cubicles installed between the walls. The crowded lairs are infested with drugs, alcohol, daggers and pistols. Cramped conditions and minimal supervision provide the *sicario* with an ideal environment to ply his trade.

Bellavista National Jail is a microcosm of Medellín's violent culture, concentrated and intensified. If a *sicario*'s chances of survival on the street are slim, his chances plummet once confined to jail. In prison, practised killers dispatch one another for money, revenge or simple amusement with terrifying regularity. During the height of Pablo Escobar's war on law enforcement, an average of 20 inmates and officers died each month inside Bellavista's walls. At times, the monthly body-count climbed as high as 50. A visiting criminologist pro-nounced it the deadliest prison in Colombia, the deadliest country in the Western world.

Bellavista evolved into a training ground for the city's killing fields. In 1986, God called Oscar Osorio to this concrete hell to announce the gospel of Jesus. The diminutive preacher began coming to Bellavista every morning at 8 o'clock to spend the day with the inmates. In fact, he spent more time with them than with his wife. She did not resent Oscar for it, however, even though she herself had to work to keep food on the table. Oscar was a Protestant preacher in an officially Roman Catholic country; his prison work was entirely voluntary. When finances got tight, he accepted temporary construction jobs to bring home a bit of cash. But the Osorios agreed that he do this only as a last resort because his true vocation was preaching to prisoners. His wife supported his ministry because, like Oscar, she believed the inmates in Bellavista deserved a chance to hear the gospel.

Nothing, not even the orgy of murder raging inside Bellavista, was going to stop Oscar Osorio from obeying God's call to preach to prisoners. The man was 100 per cent committed to the task of sharing God's love with inmates who played football with human heads. That was because he himself loved every last one of them.

2

Death Culture

When asked to explain why theirs is the Western world's most violent nation, Colombians sometimes answer by telling this fanciful parable.

> In the days of creation, God announced to the angels that he was going to create a very special country. 'This is how it will be,' he said. 'Two oceans, the balmy Caribbean and the mighty Pacific, will bathe its shores. The heavens will provide warm winds and abundant rainfall, so that it will never know ice or snow or drought. I shall fashion a great, tropical plain in the east, where immense herds of cattle will graze. In the west, broad rivers will flow between verdant mountain ranges. Rich soils shall produce the world's finest coffee and all manner of food crops. The forests will shelter many species of animals and exotic birds. Under the ground I shall sow precious metals, oil and emeralds. The name of this country shall be called "Colombia".'
>
> The astonished angels gasped. 'But, Lord, such a land will truly be a paradise. What of the countries round about? They will be jealous of Colombia and say that you were not fair.'
>
> 'I shall be fair,' God replied, 'because I shall populate this special country with . . . Colombians.'

Every thoughtful Colombian has pondered the question of why their land, so favoured by geography and so wealthy in natural resources, sheds so much blood. Ill temper is obviously not the cause. Colombians are an amiable race. Men are as well-mannered as they are well-groomed. Women are coy and lovely. Among Latin Americans, who are known for warmth and hospitality, Colombians are the warmest and most hospitable. A friend who spent several holidays in Colombia, while her husband was posted to Venezuela with the Foreign Office, fell in love with the people. She later told me, 'I really don't think I would mind if a Colombian shot me dead, because he would be so nice about it.'

Colombia's gracious ambience defies attempts to explain why murder happens so often there. Violence theories abound, but none seem to account for the complexities of what Colombians refer to as their peculiar 'culture of death'.

Certainly history has played a part in the evolution of the death culture. During the wars of independence from Spain, opposing generals decreed a battlefield policy of taking no prisoners. Captured troops were summarily executed, along with civilians caught aiding the enemy. The ruthless tactic, first mandated by none other than the Great Liberator Simón Bolívar himself, was meant to terrorize the enemy into submission. Instead, the atrocities nourished hatreds and unleashed a cycle of vengeance.

The legacy of political retaliation resurfaced in the mid-twentieth century, when Colombia suffered a prolonged period of civil turmoil known as *La Violencia*. In 1948, an unknown assailant murdered the popular Liberal politician Jorge Gaitán on a Bogotá street in broad daylight. After beating the assassin to death, Gaitán's enraged followers launched a spontaneous riot, burning and looting the capital for days. The madness swept to other cities and towns.

The mood of the entire country turned malevolent. Over the next decade, political parties, business magnates, workers' unions and security forces brutally competed to assert their will over an unruly society. None could restore peace. By the early 1960s, when *La Violencia* is presumed to have ceased, 200,000 lives had been sacrificed.

La Violencia, in fact, lives on. Present-day rebel movements like the Revolutionary Armed Forces of Colombia, which goes by the Spanish acronym FARC, and the Army of National

Liberation or ELN, are the only serious guerrilla armies remaining in Latin America. They fight both the official army and paramilitary death squads. The origins of the conflict hark back to the troubled 1950s. About the only recourse peasant farmers had to survive the political cannibalism Liberals and Conservatives were inflicting on one another was to ally themselves with local warlords. During the 1960s, these guerrilla bands metamorphosed, thanks to a bit of inspiration from Fidel Castro, into Marxist revolutionaries.

*   *   *

In June 1951, Gerardo Pino stood with his parents on the edge of a grassy airstrip waiting for the munitions plane to land. They had decided to leave Salgar, in the mountains of Antioquia and home to the Pino family for generations. They were not the only ones. A score of anxious adults and wide-eyed children waited with them for the plane, which would bear them to safety after Liberal soldiers finished unloading its cargo of guns and bullets. The guerrilla commander, Captain Reyes, had authorized passage for the Pino family because their sons and cousins fought with him in the Liberal army.

Gerardo himself had not joined the guerrillas, but he had helped supply them with guns. Smuggling was one of several crafts he had learned since leaving home seven years before.

He was 13 then. He left because he was tired of wearing hand-me-down clothing from his three elder brothers, and so set out to seek his fortune. His first job in the coffee fields earned Gerardo only two *centavos* a day and a bed, but he could live well on that at age 13. After a year in the coffee fields, he decided he wanted to live better.

With a friend named Manuel, he learned a new craft: assault and robbery. In the beginning, they practised petty thievery, shaking down strangers on the streets of Bogotá, Manizales, Buenaventura, Cali and Pereira. The teenagers moved often to keep ahead of the law. Eventually they formed a gang of seven artful dodgers and graduated to bigger targets:

shops, lorries and the riverboats that plied the broad Magdalena. When he returned home at 17, Gerardo was wearing a brand-new suit of clothes intended to impress his parents.

A year later he joined the Colombian army and was assigned cavalry duty in the Guajira peninsula. The posting allowed him to learn a new craft, fraud. Gerardo served as an aid to the officer in charge of issuing border passes. The documents sold at a premium to smugglers moving contraband across the Venezuela border. Gerardo knew the drawer in which his commander kept the passes, the hour at which he customarily left the office and the names of the smugglers who would pay him premium prices for a forged pass.

Gerardo was still serving in the Guajira when *La Violencia* struck. His skills in subterfuge were soon put to the service of the Liberal cause, running guns to guerrillas. Instinct told him it was time to move on to keep ahead of the law, so he left the army and rejoined his family back in Salgar.

Like many poor farmers, the Pinos were Liberals, which made them sworn enemies of the *chumos*, secret militias organized by the Conservatives and armed by the police to fight the Liberals. Gerardo listened to whispered tales of *chumo* atrocities. Riverboat crews told of headless corpses floating down the Magdalena, casualties of upstream mayhem. Neighbours described how *chumos* in police uniforms ambushed an entire family on a country road. After killing the adults, they tossed the infants and small children in the air and practised catching them on bayonets.

The atrocities did not involve only the Pino family's neighbours. Before it was over, *La Violencia* would claim the life of eight of Gerardo's relatives: uncles, cousins, a brother-in-law and his maternal grandfather. Most of the casualties were men, two of whom served in Captain Reyes's guerrilla army. But none died more cruelly than Gerardo's first cousin, Carolina.

She and her husband, Julio, lived in a secluded farmhouse with their three small children. Carolina was pregnant with their fourth child. One night the *chumos* caught the young couple alone on a path near their home. The killers split open

Carolina's womb, removed her unborn child and stuffed it into a gaping hole cut into Julio's body cavity. Relatives never learned why the couple had been chosen for execution, or why the Conservatives ordered their henchmen to desecrate the bodies, except perhaps to humiliate their Liberal enemies and terrorize them into submission. It did not work.

A low drone signalled the arrival of the munitions plane. The group of anxious adults and wide-eyed children pressed forward to catch a glimpse of the aircraft. It landed and disgorged its cargo of guns and bullets for Captain Reyes's Liberal soldiers. Cousins and brothers shook hands, said goodbyes, hugged their sisters and mothers. The craft took off again, carrying Gerardo Pino, his parents and siblings away from the carnage in Salgar to a city of refuge. Its name was Medellín.

*   *   *

As turbulent as Colombia's political history has been, it cannot fully account for the country's obsession with violence. Civil wars have torn many other societies apart. The mid-nineteenth-century North–South conflict in the United States, for example, killed 600,000 Americans, more casualties than the country has suffered in all other wars combined, including both world wars. Yet, when that civil war was over, the killing stopped. Why does it drag on in Colombia?

Many thoughtful Colombians say that poverty has bred the death culture. Young men reared on peasant homesteads or in dismal slums turn to careers terrorists or *sicarios* to better their lot in life. *Pistoleros* are a necessary evil in an economy like Colombia's, some say. They point out that a tiny minority owns a lion's share of the land and capital. The wide disparity between rich and poor means the élite classes must maintain well-armed security squads to protect them from the professional bandits who prey on their wealth. Eliminate poverty in Colombia, the theory goes, and you will eliminate violence.

The weakness of this argument is that poverty, despair and injustice do not seem to breed widespread violence in other Latin American countries. Bolivia, a not-too-distant neighbour midway down the Andes mountain range, is one example. The average Bolivian earns less than half the annual income of his counterpart in Colombia, about one-tenth of what a US citizen earns. One in every two Bolivians lives below the poverty line. In 1995, the United Nations Index of Human Development, which rates factors like nutrition, literacy, health and life expectancy, ranked Bolivia 113th out of the 174 countries of the world in quality of life. Colombia was placed a respectable 57th, just four places below the world's largest Spanish-speaking nation, Mexico.

If widespread poverty were a dependable indicator of violence in society, Bolivia should be a powder keg ready to explode in class warfare. Really? It is true that the country has a reputation for political instability. However, attempts at armed rebellion, like Che Guevara's 1969 foray into Bolivia to introduce Cuban-style reforms, tend to sputter from lack of interest. Bolivians sometimes refer to the revolution of 1952, which profoundly restructured their society, as the Holy Week Revolution. The shooting commenced on Good Friday and ended on Easter Sunday.

Homicide is not unknown in Bolivia, but occurs rarely. In fact, you are five times more likely to be murdered in New York City, among the most affluent citizens of the Western Hemisphere, than you are mingling with the poorest in La Paz. In 1996, La Paz police registered 29 homicides. Medellín suffers that many murders every 36 hours. Colombia's national homicide rate is 11 times that of the United States, 23 times that of Bolivia. Among its population of 32 million, 80 violent deaths occur every day, 28,000 every year. Poverty alone cannot account for such carnage.

Medellín, March 1997

A young mother lies in the darkness of a modest home in Medellín weeping quietly. Luz Dary Donado strokes the curly tresses of her three-year-old daughter, Laura Cristina, sleeping beside her and thinks back over the heartbreak of the past few days.

Less than a month ago, she was sleeping with Walter in their own bedroom across town. Her husband was completing studies to become a dental hygienist. The couple were active in youth ministries at their church, and Walter served as an elder. He also led a Christian discipleship class in their neighbourhood.

One afternoon Walter surprised a band of teenagers stealing oranges from a tree in the backyard. He reminded the young fellows that the tree had an owner. Furthermore, they did not have to steal the fruit, he would give them all they wanted.

The delinquents resented Mr Donado's reprimand. At noon the next day, Walter walked down to the corner shop to buy ice cream for Laura Cristina. He never returned. Juan Carlos, a 16-year-old gang member, was waiting for him with a home-made pipe gun loaded with black powder and metal scraps. Juan Carlos shot Walter in the face at point-blank range.

A neighbour came running to give Luz Dary the terrible news. She and Walter's brother, Nelson, rushed to the corner and found the wounded man unconscious. They carried him to the hospital and waited together through the nine-hour surgery. They prayed fervently that God would sustain Walter's life. He did not. The 31-year-old dental hygienist and church elder died at 2 o'clock the following morning.

Walter's parents arrived from Bogotá and held an anguished family council. They faced a serious problem. Police had come to the hospital and questioned Luz Dary and Nelson about the murderer and his accomplices. But the officers failed to arrest any of the gang members. Now Walter's killers threatened the Donado family with retaliation for reporting the murder to the authorities.

A few days after the murder, Luz Dary encountered one of the youths on the street. 'You're going to weep! You're going to weep! Boom, boom, boom!' he taunted her in a sing-song voice. Luz Dary had no choice but to move out of her house. She took Laura Cristina and went to live with her mother on the other side of town.

A trusted friend arranged a telephone conference with the leader of the teenage gang and asked him to halt the vendetta against the grieving family. The youth replied cryptically, 'I advise you not to get involved.'

The friend called Luz Dary. 'For your own safety, you had better stay away from your house,' he told her. 'Anybody in this country in your predicament has to do that. You never know how far these guys will go. The law of impunity reigns.'

Two weeks later, and escorted by police, Nelson returned to Luz Dary's apartment to retrieve some family belongings. They found the place ransacked. The intruders, evidently the same youths who murdered Walter, had stolen the stereo, some records, the coffee maker and other household appliances. They also leafed through the family photo album and removed pictures. This frightened Luz Dary most. Killers stole photographs to identify future victims. So that no one would doubt their intentions, the thugs left a note with a pointed message for the Donado family: 'You sons of b——s have two weeks to clear everything out of here, or you die.'

The church was doing what it could. A spokesman had issued a public statement, asking believers to pray for the safety of the Donado family and asking God to use Walter's death to bring others to faith in God. Fellow Christians had called to express sympathy and offer help. Yet they knew that, beyond prayer, there was little anyone could do for the young widow and her child.

So Luz Dary lay in the darkness of her mother's guest room, cradled her three-year-old daughter in her arms and wept. Through her tears, she prayed. 'God, I know you have the right over life and death. But why Walter? He had so much to offer.'

The young widow stroked Laura Cristina's curly tresses for some moments more, before adding, 'Please, God, make this nightmare end.'

*   *   *

The poverty-breeds-violence theory founders on the fact that some of Colombia's most successful businessmen are some of its deadliest killers. In only twenty years, entrepreneurs based in Antioquia and Valle, two states known for their robust economies, have developed a new industry that produces billions of dollars a year in revenue: the drug cartel.

These wildly successful business ventures have forged international marketing networks. The profits they generate through high-volume sales of marijuana and cocaine have enriched untold numbers of Colombians. What is more, the cartels have benefited poor people in other countries of Latin America, including thousands of peasant farmers in Bolivia, who supplement their meagre incomes by growing coca leaf, the raw material from which cocaine is extracted.

An obvious problem for the industry is that the commercialization of marijuana and cocaine is illegal. Powerful countries in North America and Europe have mounted massive interdiction efforts. Their aim is to dismantle the cartels' marketing networks and, ultimately, drive the industry out of business. The fierce contest between drug traffickers and law enforcement has ignited yet another violent conflict within Colombia: the drug war.

The drug war has received a great deal of attention from the mass media in North America and Europe in recent years, which is understandable, given the collective national interests at stake and the huge amounts of public funds committed to combat illicit drugs. Press reports in the USA and Europe often give the impression that drugs have turned Colombia into a violent nation, thus lending credibility to the drugs-breed-violence theory. However, this explanation does no better than others in getting at the root causes of the death culture. In fact, only about a sixth of the homicides committed in Colombia each year are drug-related. One can just as well argue that the culture of death bred the drug war as insist that drugs gave birth to violence in Colombia.

Medellín, March 1993

Juan Carlos Londoño, alias Juan Caca, crawled under a car parked in the enclosed yard of a small house in Medellín. The

22-year-old needed only to connect a few more wires and the vehicle would be ready to go. Juan and Fernando Acosta, Ñangas as he was known to his colleagues in the Medellín drug cartel, planned to drive the car to Cali. This was no normal auto, however, nor would their trip be a casual excursion. Juan and Ñangas had strapped hundreds of sticks of dynamite to the undercarriage and interior panels of the car and planned to detonate the explosives on a busy street in the heart of Cali.

Car bombs were Juan Caca's criminal speciality. Born into a working-class family, he dropped out of his first year of secondary school to work for his father. Yearning to earn real money, he joined a gang of neighbourhood thugs and began robbing up-market shops and burgling fancy homes. He did not consider stealing from the rich a sin. He did feel pangs of guilt the first time he had to kill, but eventually mastered his conscience so that even murder, under certain circumstances, became acceptable.

Juan Caca was good enough at his craft to attract the attention of wealthy criminals. The Medellín cartel contracted him to build car bombs and plot the assassination of police officers. By then, he had mastered his conscience to the point that he did not consider those crimes a sin, either. They were simply offensive operations in a war, the drug war.

Juan Caca's commanding officer was Pablo Escobar, the founder and lord of the Medellín drug cartel. Recently Escobar had ordered his troops to step up assaults on public officials and rival drug traffickers. Escobar was in the fight of his life. Enemies in the Cali cartel wanted to eliminate him and were feeding intelligence to the security forces. Colombia's top lawman, Gustavo De Greiff, had personally assumed oversight of the manhunt for Escobar and was tightening the noose about him. The drug lord had nearly resigned himself to defeat. However, a condition of his surrender was government permission for his wife and children to emigrate to Europe, a condition public officials flatly rejected. That's why Juan Caca and Ñangas were building the car bomb. When detonated, it would send a double message: a warning to the Cali cartel to stand down and a demand for the government to give Escobar his way.

This was not the first bomb Juan Caca had built for the drug lord. Six weeks before, he received orders to plant a car bomb in the parking garage of the Chamber of Commerce in Bogotá. When he and a companion arrived there, the garage was closed, so they drove around the block to park in front of the building. The parking spots were all occupied. Time was running out. Londoño was sweating. They pulled over to the kerb. 'Let's leave it here,' he hissed. 'We can't wait any longer!'

The two managed to get out of range before the detonator activated. The bomb blasted an enormous crater in the street and filled the air with acrid smoke. Bodies lay strewn among hulks of burning cars. Screams and sobs echoed from blackened apartment buildings, their windows blown out by the blast. Severed electrical lines shot sparks at rescuers. The injured and dying inundated area hospitals. Twenty corpses were taken to the morgue. Three of the dead were toddlers. Yuri Marcela, 11 months old, would never know she had become a casualty of the drug war.

Survivors would rebuild their lives slowly. The wounded underwent surgery to repair shattered limbs and charred flesh. Families moved out of their apartments and into temporary shelters. Some depleted life savings to rebuild damaged homes or replace destroyed cars. Mothers grieved for dead children, fathers worried about paying unexpected bills. Everyone asked why. Why did they do it?

Juan Caca did it for the money. He kept a storage chest in the small house in Medellín filled with sticks of dynamite and bundles of US dollar bills. The money provided the usual perks of his profession: high-performance motorcycles, lavish apartments, fine clothes for his girlfriends. On this day, the chest contained $15,000 in cash. Of course, Juan Caca had earned many times that amount from his criminal speciality. Gustavo De Greiff had pieced together evidence linking Londoño to the deaths of some 150 people. A few were police officers, rival drug traffickers and other enemy troops in the drug war. The vast majority were innocent civilians, like Yuri Marcela.

Deep inside, Londoño conceded that he built car bombs

because he had no other choice. If he refused to obey cartel orders, he would become a casualty of the drug war himself. Juan Caca had reached the pinnacle of the cartel hierarchy. Pablo Escobar had admitted him into his inner circle. That circle exercised ruthless power and enjoyed unimaginable wealth, but knew nothing of compassion, pity or pardon.

Londoño did not think about dying while he prepared the car bomb for Cali. It might have interfered with his concentration. Nor did he think about the other fate that might befall him, prison. In some ways, that was a fate worse than death. Police officers would torture him, seeking sensitive information about cartel operations. If he revealed the information, cartel colleagues would retaliate by torturing and murdering his loved ones. Like most *sicarios,* Londoño preferred death to jail.

Juan connected the wires and crawled out from under the car. He and Ñangas inspected the vehicle and discussed their final plans. Then they walked out of the enclosed yard and up the street to meet three cartel colleagues. They never made it.

Suddenly, armed strangers surrounded them on the pavement and pointed guns directly at their heads. Juan froze. A sickening thought flashed through his mind: 'This is it. I'm going to die.'

'Put your hands above your heads!' one of the strangers barked. 'You are under arrest.'

Bogotá, October 1992

Dr Mario Madrid Malo was in his office at the Guillermo Cano Institute on Human Rights, talking with a journalist about drugs and violence. Despite the fact that the Cano Institute is named in honour of a newspaper editor whom the Medellín cartel assassinated in 1986 for his outspoken opposition to drug trafficking, Madrid Malo does not blame drugs for fomenting the death culture. His staff has compiled comprehensive statistics on murder in Colombia that point to many different causes.

'Violence in Colombia assumes a variety of forms,' he said.

'We don't just have insurgent violence, or the violence perpetrated by military personnel who abuse their power, or the violence of drug traffickers, we also have the violence of common crime. All these forms of violence have created not only the culture of death, but something worse: the triviality of death. Unfortunately for us, murder is no longer news.'

'No longer news' means the Colombian press reports only one in ten of the eighty murders committed each day. Police investigate only one in three. Records from the Attorney General's Office show that 97 per cent of criminals are never brought to justice.

'Even more dramatic,' Madrid Malo added, 'is violence in the family.' Then he, like every thoughtful Colombian, expounded his own theory of the death culture. He thinks it starts at home.

*   *   *

Oscar Osorio can't remember how old he was when he started hating God, but he remembers it was on a Christmas morning. Ernesto and Genoveva seldom talked to their 17 children about God, except on Christmas Eve. Then they told them they must go to bed early because the Christ Child would be coming through the neighbourhood leaving gifts for all the good children. If he were to arrive and find them still awake, he would go on to other houses and leave their gifts for other children.

So Oscar and his siblings lay down side by side on their burlap sacks to await the Christ Child. He never came. The Osorio children found no gifts on Christmas mornings in their one-room house in Villa Hermosa. That was why Oscar started hating God. He thought God must hate him, as well.

Oscar's father did not hate him, but the young boy could not be sure he loved him either. As his family grew larger, Ernesto felt the added pressure of providing for them. The stress kept him away from home more often to gamble and drink. When he did come back, he had little more than hard blows and harsh words for Genoveva and the children.

One night when Oscar was nine, he stood with his brothers and sisters on the pavement in front of the Osorio house desperately hoping his father would come home. The family had not seen Ernesto for three days. They had subsisted on bread and *panela* water, dreaming of a hearty *sancocho* made with manioc, potatoes and plantains. About 11 o'clock, the children saw their father coming up the street with a bulging burlap sack on his shoulder.

'Papa's coming! Papa's coming!' they announced to a weary Genoveva, who was once again pregnant. She set them to kindling a fire and putting water in the kettle. The Osorio children giggled with delight and hugged Ernesto around the knees. Then they set to work peeling the vegetables.

The savoury aroma of the *sancocho* was just beginning to waft from the kettle when a fierce argument broke out in the one-room house at the back of the dirt lot. Genoveva was screaming and crying, Ernesto was shouting and slapping her. The children trembled with dread. 'Papa is beating mama! Papa is beating mama!' they whispered to one another.

Ernesto exploded from the house, still in a rage. 'Out of my way you sons of b——es, you little gonorrhoeas!' he bellowed at the children. The kids scrambled to avoid their father's punches and kicks. Ernesto continued to curse them. He spied the pot of *sancocho*, just beginning to boil. The children watched in horror as he grabbed the handle of the pot and swung it in a wide arc, scattering half-cooked manioc, potatoes and plantains to the far corners of the dirt lot. He hurled the empty kettle on the ground, stomped out of the front gate and disappeared.

Oscar and his brothers looked at each other, stunned and silent. They listened to their mother sobbing back in the one-room house and to their sisters whimpering from fright. Then their attention turned back to the *sancocho*. Wearily they retrieved the pot, refilled it with water and rekindled the fire. They began searching the dark patio by the flickering light, picking up the scattered vegetables, washing off the dirt and carefully replacing them in the simmering pot. It was difficult work, especially when one's stomach ached from hunger and one's eyes filled with salty tears.

Oscar Osorio already hated God. That night he learned to hate his father as well.

*   *   *

'It is said, with little humour, that beating your wife is a national sport in Colombia,' Madrid Malo was telling the journalist in his office. 'Violence against children assumes two severe forms: sexual abuse and cruel and inhuman treatment. This violence in the bosom of the domestic household clearly speaks of an alarming underdevelopment of the conscience.'

The conscience. Whether he was talking about the human conscience or the national conscience, Madrid Malo had put his finger on the root cause of the death culture in Colombia. Whatever history or economics or sociology has to do with it, murder does not happen on the street until the murderer can justify his appalling action in his own mind.

So the search for a theory to explain why Colombia is the most violent nation in the Western world comes back to the fanciful parable about creation. In telling it, Colombians do not accuse God of discrimination against their homeland. They are only admitting that violence is ultimately a pathology of the spirit, be it the human spirit or the national spirit. One of their poets, Gonzalo Arango, stated it most eloquently when he wrote his wistful lament: 'Is there not some way that Colombia, instead of killing its sons, can make them worthy to live?'

3

Encounters with the Lord

One day in September 1983, 28-year-old Oscar Osorio was sleeping off another drug binge on a pavement in Villa Hermosa. He had lain there on a sheet of cardboard for three days in a semiconscious stupor. The drug that put him there was not the marijuana or pills or *cacao sabanero* he had known since childhood.

A friend had introduced him to the potent substance one night after Oscar had moved back to Medellín from Barranquilla. They were drinking together in a tavern when the fellow took a small lump of coffee-coloured paste from his pocket, scraped a bit into a cigarette and lit it for Oscar. As soon as the smoke hit his sinuses, Oscar knew he wanted more of that coffee-coloured paste.

His friend told him the name, *bazuco*. It came from the residue left in the bottom of tubs used to refine cocaine. Bazuco was cheap and plentiful. Oscar wanted more. Within a few weeks, bazuco had become the centre of his life. He cared only to steal and deal enough to buy some more of the coffee-coloured paste. While the drug was in his bloodstream, Oscar did not care to eat or sleep or bathe. Nor did he think about his family or his crimes or the emptiness down at the bottom of his soul.

He did think about those things when he was in prison. Jail terms always caused Oscar to meditate on his childhood in the one-room house with his parents and 16 brothers and sisters. He had concluded that no one in this world loved him. Not his mother, nor his father, nor his brothers and sisters, not even Estela. Oscar loved no one, not even himself. He often sat in the jail cell pondering how to commit suicide. But even that thought brought little comfort because he knew he lacked the courage to kill himself. He could not endure his life and could not imagine life ever improving.

Another curious thing happened to Oscar when he was in jail. He turned religious. He still hated God, of course, but he prayed regularly to the Virgin Mary. He also invoked the *animus* of his grandmother. His parents told him what a saintly woman she had been and encouraged him to call upon her spirit in purgatory whenever he needed help. Oscar attended Mass in the prison chapel and went to confession. He was candid with the priest, admitting his crimes and fornications and drug abuse. He repented of his bad deeds and did penance as instructed. Still he felt the nagging emptiness at the bottom of his soul. Once he left prison, he always returned to his bad deeds.

So Oscar was lying on his sheet of cardboard that September day when a man named Jairo Chalarca walked by with a Bible under his arm. Chalarca paused, looked at Oscar and said: 'Jesus loves you and he wants to change your life.'

Those words somehow penetrated the cloud in Oscar's head. 'What did you say?'

'Jesus loves you and he will change your life,' Chalarca repeated.

Oscar stared at the stranger. No one had ever said words like that to him before, but they intrigued him. He had heard the name 'Jesus', of course, but never had it sounded quite like it did coming from this man's lips.

Chalarca noticed a flicker of interest in the young man's face. He kept talking, telling Oscar that he was important, that God had plans for him, plans far better than sleeping on a cardboard sheet on the street. Oscar listened. 'Would you like to come with me to church?' Chalarca asked. 'I'm on my way there now.'

'I can't walk into a church like this,' Oscar said. 'I haven't had a bath in weeks. My clothes are filthy. I need a haircut.'

'That doesn't matter,' Chalarca said. 'Please, come with me.'

Oscar got up and walked with the man a few blocks to the Covenant Evangelical Church of Villa Hermosa. He had never been inside the building before that day. He had never been inside any Protestant church before that day. He took a seat and watched his companion walk to the front and mount the platform. Jairo Chalarca, the pastor of the Covenant Evangelical Church, preached the sermon that day.

Afterwards, Oscar could not remember the text of Scripture Pastor Chalarca expounded nor any of the stories he narrated. He did hear the pastor say this: 'God knows you. God loves you. God will take on your problems if you turn them over to him. God will take over your life if you turn it over to him.'

As Pastor Chalarca spoke, Oscar began to cry. This was a most remarkable thing because Oscar had not wept for years. He began to feel something change at the bottom of his soul. At the end of the sermon, he heard Pastor Chalarca say, 'Jesus Christ knows you. He knows exactly what condition you are in. If you come to know Christ, he will raise you up. He will change your life. If you want to meet Christ today, come forward to the front of the church and we will pray with you.'

Oscar quickly walked to the front of the church, brushing tears from his eyes. 'I want this life you are talking about,' he said to Pastor Chalarca. 'I want to know Jesus.'

Jairo placed his hands on Oscar's shoulders and began to pray. Afterwards, Oscar could not quite put into words what happened to him during that prayer, but it was something like this: he felt the sensation of tons of weight bearing down on him. He could not get out from under it. The weight was tormenting, suffocating him. Suddenly the crushing weight lifted off his body. He felt buoyant, strong, calm, relaxed. He felt free.

He was free. After that prayer, Oscar Osorio never again smoked *bazuco* or marijuana or sniffed cocaine. After that prayer, he never robbed another shop nor picked another pocket nor put a knife to another throat. After that prayer, he never again committed fraud or fornication. He was free.

Oscar no longer felt empty. 'It felt like something had broken my heart and carried away the bitterness,' he said afterwards. 'Something tore out all my desire for wrongful pleasure. I felt an inward peace that I had never before experienced.'

'It all happened in an instant. And when it was over, I didn't hate God any more.'

In fact, Oscar did not hate anybody any more. He went home and told his mother that he wanted to change, no, that he had changed. He asked if it would be all right if he moved back into the house. Genoveva was sceptical, but agreed. Oscar shaved and showered and cut off his shaggy hair. A few days later, he got a job bricklaying. A few days after that, he came home with a parcel of groceries, groceries he had actually purchased with honest wages. That was the day Genoveva Osorio knew that her son had indeed changed.

Medellín, January 1994

'My life began sadly with a hard-headed father and a superstitious mother. My dad taught me to come home drunk and mop up the house with the wife. He beat us kids and made us endure hunger. He was a wealthy man, but gave us nothing. From six years of age, my dream was to make money, it did not matter how, so that I could humiliate my father and one day, perhaps kill him.'

Orlando Taborda, 34, is speaking. He is a man of medium build, caramel skin, coffee-coloured eyes and Afro curly hair. He sits back in the overstuffed chair and narrates his personal history.

By age 12, I was living with a girlfriend. I started as a swindler, passing counterfeit bills, writing bad cheques, learning every kind of fraud. I worked at this about seven years before starting to use drugs. I had no other thought in mind than making money, no matter who it harmed.

I believed that happiness came with women, cars and bank accounts. By 15, I was a father. I wanted nothing of the responsibility, so I abandoned the girl. After doing more damage to other people, I married. I probably did the most damage to my wife. I abused her verbally and physically in every way imaginable. I even tried three times to kill her with a firearm, besides trying several other times with a knife. Once I tried to hang her with a bed sheet. I beat her constantly and that would send her home to her mother. My father had taught me to behave like this and, well, I was pretty good at it.

By the time my daughter Natalia was three, I wanted desperately to get off drugs. I begged my wife for forgiveness and she decided to help. She enrolled me in Alcoholics Anonymous and I stopped drinking and doing drugs. But my mind was unchanged. I still had the ambition to make lots of money.

About that time a man said to me: 'Look, Orlando, I know you are a man capable of murder. Now that you are not doing drugs any more, I need you to work with me.' That was my life ambition, so I said yes. I had already killed some people, but only those who upset me. I had never killed for pay.

At 23 years of age, I started working for organized crime. The first time they hired me, it was to kidnap five Colombians and a Peruvian from the Intercontinental Hotel in Bogotá. Another fellow and I went in and quietly captured them. They were armed, but we surprised them and took away their guns. The people who contracted me were quite happy with the work because just two of us were able to take six of them. I earned $70,000 dollars and a reputation.

Clients started contracting me to kill. I formed my own *sicario* company. I hired nine men and two women. We had offices in Medellín and Bogotá. We worked the whole country committing assassinations, transporting drugs, kidnapping – whatever jobs the Mafia or some government official needed us to do.

In Medellín, when they want to kill somebody who's not important, they hire a kid from the slums. When they want to kill some tough *mafioso*, they hire specialized *sicarios* who charge big fees. I was a specialist.

For this type of work, you have to have a plan. You follow the person for a period of time, watching where he hangs out. You synchronize your schedules, calculate distances to streets you can use for escape. After that, it's a matter of waiting until he turns up. On some jobs, the two women who worked for us would crash their car into his. Our *sicarios* are riding on the floor of the vehicle, and when he gets out with his bodyguards to check the damage, they shoot them all. The women take off in one car with the guns, the fellows flee in another car. Later we meet at some tavern in town to celebrate.

In the underworld, when they talk to you about a homicide, they say: 'How much will you charge to kill this person? Twenty million pesos?' And you begin to picture what 20 million pesos will buy. It motivates you to kill. The first money you earn goes to buy weapons and cars, to show off the quality of work you do. In the beginning, you don't see death or jail. No. You see property.

*   *   *

Carmenza Perez grew up in Villa Hermosa across the street from Oscar Osorio, but she might as well have lived on another planet. Her father earned good wages in the hardwood flooring business and provided a comfortable living for his wife, Mery, and their two children. Carmenza and her younger brother never lacked food or clothing or shoes. They slept in beds and studied in private schools. What little Carmenza knew about the Osorios, the *bonboneros* as Mery Perez called them, she overheard from her mother.

'Every neighbourhood has to have one family like *them*, I suppose. The worst of the lot is that boy, Oscar. Smokes marijuana and who knows what else.'

Carmenza had never met Oscar Osorio, who was 12 years her senior, but heard once that he had gone off to live in Barranquilla and who knows where else.

Not long after Carmenza graduated from secondary school a girlfriend invited her to worship services at the Covenant Evangelical Church. Carmenza found the music enjoyable, the preaching stimulating and the believers' trust in God to arrange personal matters intriguing. The first time she tried this herself, praying that God would provide her with suitable employment, her prayer was answered within the week. That experience convinced her to trust God to arrange a greater matter, her own salvation. Carmenza prayed what the believers called the prayer of faith. Soon afterwards, she asked Jairo Chalarca to baptize her.

Carmenza invited her mother to attend church with her. Mery Perez accepted and found that she, too, enjoyed the worship services. She began attending regularly with her daughter, although she did not pray the prayer of faith. 'It is all very well that we go to this church,' Mrs Perez told her daughter. 'The singing is lovely and the Bible teaching is sound. But don't ever marry an evangelical. Evangelicals are always poor.'

The Covenant Evangelical Church intrigued Mery Perez because she saw Oscar Osorio there. Mothers all over Villa Hermosa were talking about the change that had come over him. He no longer slept on the streets or sold marijuana to their children. Rather, he worked every day as a bricklayer, went about clean-shaven and sober and spent nearly every spare minute at the church studying Scripture with Pastor Chalarca.

From the moment he met Jesus, Oscar began to feel a compelling urge to do something, anything, for God. He did not aspire to the important tasks of the ministry, teaching and preaching and such, because he had never learned to read and write. But he did want to do something. He started with what he could do, sweeping the sanctuary, cleaning the toilets, washing windows. Jairo Chalarca noted Oscar's willingness to work and gave him opportunities to do other chores for the Lord. He called on Oscar to lead public prayer, to help serve the Lord's Supper and to lead informal choruses in the worship service. Eventually, he invited him to help counsel the many teenagers who were coming to know Jesus at the Covenant Evangelical Church.

That is how Oscar Osorio met Carmenza Perez. One day she asked him to pray with her about a very personal matter – a boyfriend. She wanted God to lead her to a suitable husband. Oscar promised he would pray, adding how important it was to seek God's guidance on the issue. He himself was engaged to be married to a girl in the church, he explained, and had benefited greatly from prayer and the counsel of Pastor Chalarca.

Carmenza did not expect God to answer her prayer quite so suddenly or unexpectedly. She was sitting in church at her mother's side while Oscar Osorio led the informal choruses, when she heard the voice of God say to her: 'That person standing up front, the one leading the choruses, he is the man who will be your husband.'

Carmenza gasped. 'No, Lord, it can't be!' she protested inwardly. 'Not him!'

'Yes, he is the one.'

'But, he already has a fiancée. Besides, he's not my type. I'm not even attracted to him. I've always wanted somebody that's, well . . . better.'

Carmenza preferred to think her imagination was playing tricks on her. But try as she might, she could not deny the fact that she had heard the voice of God.

*   *   *

Gerardo Pino passed a milestone in his life in 1951, the year he escaped *La Violencia* on Captain Reyes's munitions plane. In 1951, he celebrated his 21st birthday, settled in Medellín and began his criminal career in earnest.

The lean, lanky young man made friends easily. They were the type of friends who liked to drink *aguardiente*, smoke marijuana and stage an occasional hold-up to finance their simple diversions. A dozen of them formed a gang, invested in some handguns and began pursuing greater diversions.

The gang specialized in robbing buses and lorries on rural roads and jewellery shops and banks in the city. Gerardo Pino learned the locksmith trade and became adept at cracking safes. A skilled professional, he spurned explosives (too messy) and stethoscope (too tedious) in favour of a high-speed drill. Pino had studied strong boxes and could, in a matter of minutes, pierce the locking mechanism at the exact point which disengaged the tumblers inside and opened the door.

The technique earned him and his fellow gang members a comfortable living. Pino bought a small farm in Planeta Rica, a town in the tropics near the Caribbean coast. He lived there with a series of girlfriends whom he took on holidays to San Andres Island to drink *aguardiente* and smoke marijuana.

All was not perfect, however. Their crimes ultimately earned Pino and his fellow gang members prison terms. Several friends died in gun battles with police and other gangs. Of the original dozen, Gerardo was the only one who survived to middle age. Along the way, he served a total of 18 prison terms, most of them in La Ladera and Bellavista.

Pino was 57 years old when he entered Bellavista for his final prison term. The judge had given him a seven-year sentence for cracking a safe in the London Jewelry Shop in Medellín. At 57, Pino was decades older than the average Bellavista inmate, and the younger men respected him for it. They respected him for other reasons, too, one being that he had survived for so long in a dangerous business. Another reason was because he had the foulest mouth of any inmate in Bellavista. Prisoners customarily hid knives or handguns under their sheets for self-protection. Pino spurned weapons. Instead he attacked enemies with searing profanity and curses. Despite his disagreeable manners, or perhaps because of them, fellow inmates gave the veteran thief the nickname 'Papa Pino'.

Pino did not think the nickname amusing, since he had no children. He had never married any of the girlfriends he lived with on his farm in Planeta Rica. Most of his 13 brothers and sisters had married, so Pino had dozens of nieces and nephews. None of them ever visited him in jail, though. He had alienated his family years before with his disagreeable manners and foul mouth.

Very soon into his final prison term, Papa Pino began to wonder if he would survive this stay in Bellavista. The jail had turned dangerously violent. Prisoners rioted to protest at overcrowding in the cell blocks. They staged hunger strikes to protest about the bad food in the cafeteria. The troubles always seemed to end in casualties. One day 13 died. On another, eight were killed. Authorities cracked down on the mischief, taking away visiting privileges. Prisoners took guards hostage to protest. The guards, too, died. No one ever sorted out who murdered whom. The inmates who survived the killings observed a strict code of silence. Inmates who did not observe a strict code of silence did not survive the killings.

Papa Pino realized it was ruthless *caciques* who inspired the constant mischief. Every cell block was controlled by a *cacique*, or chief. He determined who had the right to a bed, who had the right to sell drugs and who had the right to kill. In reality, the only inmates who had the right to kill were the *cacique*'s associates, his *carros* as they were called. They mostly killed at his bidding.

The killing inside Bellavista, Pino realized, was about power. But as so often happens, the more the *caciques* killed, the less control they maintained. Eventually they themselves fell under the control of a sinister power, a power of death. That was why a man like Papa Pino needed a foul mouth to survive inside Bellavista. Bellavista was a foul place.

*   *   *

'Something very strange is happening to me. I'm falling in love.'

Carmenza Perez was in a dilemma. In a matter of months she had developed feelings, quite strong feelings, for Oscar Osorio. But she could admit them to no one, not to Pastor Chalarca, certainly not to her mother, not even to Oscar himself. Finally she confided in a friend at work.

'What's so strange about falling in love?' her friend said.

'But I don't want to fall in love with this man,' Carmenza replied. 'I *can't* fall in love with him. He's too old, he's too plain and he's too . . . different. Besides, he's already in love with someone else.'

'Yes, that is strange,' her friend said. 'But don't worry. Give it time and you'll get over him.'

Carmenza gave it time but did not get over Oscar. Outwardly, her relationship with him was purely platonic. She could not imagine that Oscar, who was steadily gaining more responsibilities at the Covenant Evangelical Church, had the same feelings for her that she had for him.

Christmas came around and Oscar invited Carmenza to observe an annual Medellín tradition, a stroll through the streets in the city centre to see the Christmas lights. When they arrived back at her door, he told her he had an important matter to discuss.

'Something very strange is happening to me,' Oscar said with a tremor in his voice. 'I think I'm falling in love with you.'

Carmenza gasped.

'I know this is impossible,' Oscar continued. 'We are from such different backgrounds. You, a well-educated young woman with a good job. Me, a former criminal and drug addict.' He smiled. 'Short, ugly and poor, as well. It's like the Beauty and the Beast.'

'Anyway,' Oscar said, 'I don't exactly understand all this, but I have very strong feelings for you and I thought you should know.'

Carmenza stared for a moment and said: 'Oscar, we'd better pray about this.'

Turmoil struck the Covenant Evangelical Church when Oscar and Carmenza began courting publicly. No one considered it a suitable match. Not Jairo Chalarca, who told Oscar that Carmenza, accustomed as she was to the good life, would distract him from serving the Lord in order to provide for her comfort. Not the parents of Oscar's former fiancée, who reminded him that if he really sought to do God's will, he should keep his promise to marry her. Certainly not Mery Perez. The thought of her daughter marrying a poor evangelical and the idea that God would allow such a thing so infuriated her that she immediately ceased attending the Covenant Evangelical Church.

The only one who favoured the match was the Lord. The more Oscar and Carmenza trusted him to arrange the matter, the deeper they fell in love with one another. They confirmed the old adage that opposites attract and discovered a new one: opposites complement. The time they spent together turned into personal growth sessions. Oscar taught Carmenza to fast, to pray, to memorize Scripture and apply it to life issues, all the basics of Christian discipleship. Carmenza taught Oscar to read and write.

The social pressure on the couple grew more intense with each passing month. Mery Perez marshalled all her maternal authority to dissuade her daughter from continuing her relationship with 'that *bonbonero*'. 'What about your education?' she reminded Carmenza. 'All that money we spent was wasted. You even studied with nuns, for heaven's sake! You should have learned *something*.'

Finally, Mrs Perez pronounced her ultimatum. 'All right, it's him, or us. Either you stay, or you leave.'

Carmenza told Oscar through tears of her mother's demand. How could things get so complicated in such a short time? She and Oscar had known each other less than a year. What could they possibly do?

'There really is only one solution,' Oscar told her quietly.

Carmenza stared mutely into his dark brown eyes. She loved this man, she knew that beyond a doubt. Despite outward appearances, she had seen in him something very noble, very strong, very wholesome. Most of all, she sensed God's blessing on their relationship. But if it was to end now, so let his will be done.

'What shall we do?' she asked gravely.

'Let's get married,' Oscar said.

Carmenza blinked. 'All right, let's get married.'

Bellavista National Jail, 1987

Bellavista National Jail, the deadliest prison in Colombia, was also the only one with a Protestant chapel on the premises.

The chapel was the work of Donald and Georgia Rendle, a Canadian couple who came to Colombia as missionaries. The Rendles first visited La Ladera Jail in February 1975. Georgia was a gifted vocalist, and La Ladera's governor, Dr Cardona Carvajal, asked her and Donald to form a prison glee club. The choir eventually grew to 80 voices, attracting even some of

Bellavista's guards. The Rendles' effort gained the goodwill of Governor Carvajal.

Soon after their arrival, an inmate named Nehemias Maestre introduced himself to the Rendles. 'I am a Christian,' Nehemias told them, 'and I've been praying for months that God would send someone here to tell these men about the gospel. I've even prayed that they would build an evangelical chapel in this prison. I believe you are the answer to my prayers.'

When the prison moved to Bellavista in 1976, the Rendles prevailed upon the governor's goodwill to build the chapel. Donald and Georgia raised money for building materials from friends in the Fellowship of Evangelical Baptist Churches in Canada. Nehemias Maestre helped supervise the construction. Once completed, the chapel provided a secure environment for the Rendles and their evangelical co-workers to meet with Bellavista prisoners for weekly worship, something that had never before occurred in any prison in Colombia.

Besides the Rendles, volunteers from the Salvation Army, the Association of Evangelical Ministries of Medellín and the Covenant Evangelical Church took an interest in Bellavista prisoners. Reverend Mario Mazo served as the first pastor of the Bellavista chapel. 'Mama' Lilian de Muñoz visited the jail every week to distribute shoes, clothing, soap and toothbrushes. Baptist churches supplied teachers for a Sunday school and donated books for a chapel library.

In 1979, the Rendles received an invitation from the National Director-General of Prisons, Dr Bernardo Echeverri, to expand their ministry into other prisons in Colombia. The couple moved to Bogotá, leaving Dr Manuel Rojas in charge in Medellín. Later, leadership passed to Dr Francisco Archila.

Two years later, Prison Fellowship, a volunteer organization in the United States, sent a representative to Colombia to meet Donald and Georgia Rendle. Prison Fellowship was the work of Charles Colson, a former aide to President Richard Nixon. Convicted of misconduct in the notorious Watergate affair, Colson found Jesus while in prison. The same year the Rendles began their work in Medellín, Colson formed Prison Fellowship to preach the gospel in US jails. In 1982, the Rendles affiliated with Colson's organization, and Prison Fellowship of Colombia was born.

Over the years, Prison Fellowship developed new and innovative services for the benefit of Bellavista inmates. Manuel Rojas edited a bimonthly magazine for prisoners called *Paths to Liberty*. Georgia wrote a training manual for prison workers entitled *Love Has No Bars*. Volunteers offered counselling services, taught classes in basic literacy and organized football leagues. They trained inmates in vegetable gardening, bee-keeping and other practical skills. A local evangelist named Manuel Casteñeda opened a halfway house to help inmates re-enter the job market upon their release from prison.

Besides Governor Carvajal, Prison Fellowship found another key ally on the Bellavista staff. She was Luz Elena Torres, Coordinator of the Penitentiary Pedagogical Program, 'P3' in prison shorthand. A Christian believer herself, Luz Elena recruited evangelical volunteers to teach in the P3 educational centre. Francisco Archila taught psychology. Javier and Victor Celis, two brothers from the Covenant Evangelical Mission, offered classes on the Bible.

But the volunteers of Prison Fellowship did much more than introduce new and innovative services for the benefit of Bellavista inmates. They succeeded in penetrating the darkest corner of Colombia with the light of the gospel of Jesus. That light would bring unimaginable changes to Colombia's deadliest prison.

*   *   *

Oscar's courtship of Carmenza had infuriated Mery Perez, but the couple's marriage truly enraged her. After the nuptials, her son-in-law was no longer poor, he was destitute. Carmenza became the sole family breadwinner.

That was because Oscar accepted a commission from the Covenant Evangelical Church to plant a new congregation in the borough of Twelfth of October. He and Carmenza decided that he would dedicate full-time energies to the assignment and they would live on the salary she earned as a secretary.

In fact, Carmenza insisted that they do so. 'It doesn't matter to me if things get tough, I just want you to preach the Word,' she told Oscar. 'I married a servant of God. If I'm to help him, I'll have to help however the Lord directs.'

The Lord had directed Carmenza to a position with a telephone paging service. It was a fledgling company in a new industry that offered excellent job security. The couple needed Carmenza's job security since Oscar resigned his position as bricklayer to plant the new church in Twelfth of October.

Carmenza left their modest apartment for work each morning at 7 o'clock, leaving her new husband to do the cleaning, shopping and cooking. Later, Oscar left to do church planting duties. These typically involved visiting neighbourhood homes, talking with interested persons, inviting them to worship services and leaving gospel tracts for them to read.

Actually, most days Oscar did not do typical church planting duties. Other interests distracted him. These involved sitting down on a sheet of cardboard with a drug addict and telling him that Jesus loved him and wanted to change his life. Or dropping by the places where neighbourhood homosexuals hung out to tell them the same thing. Some days Oscar would encounter a street preacher in a park or plaza and round up as many street people as he could find to come and listen. He had been doing this kind of thing ever since the day he prayed the prayer of faith with Jairo Chalarca and could not seem to break the habit.

One day Oscar collected some street people to listen to a man preaching in Bolívar Park. The preacher mentioned that his name was Manuel Casteñeda and that he operated a halfway house in Medellín for men who had recently been released from Bellavista Jail. Oscar was intrigued when Casteñeda narrated the personal histories of a few of the men who had become Christians in prison. Afterwards, Oscar introduced himself to Casteñeda. When he learned that the man regularly visited Bellavista Jail to preach, Oscar asked if he could go along. Casteñeda said he could, and promised to introduce Oscar to the director of Prison Fellowship, Francisco

Archila. Dr Archila would see to it that Oscar received a pass from the governor of Bellavista allowing him to visit the jail.

That night at dinner, Oscar and Carmenza were discussing the day. She had spent it answering telephone pages and he performing church planting duties. Oscar told of meeting Manuel Casteñeda in Bolívar Park.

'He invited me to go along to the Bellavista Jail tomorrow,' he told Carmenza.

'What for?' she asked, having no concept of what a servant of God might do in a jail.

'To preach the gospel to the prisoners,' Oscar said. 'That's all right with you, isn't it?'

'That's fine,' Carmenza replied. She had no concept of what Bellavista National Jail was like, but she knew anything that involved preaching was what her husband was meant to do. She would be glad to help him do it, however the Lord directed.

4

Bellavista

Oscar Osorio sat in the office of Fernando Bonilla, governor of Bellavista Jail. He was there to ask a favour. The governor expected it to be a small favour. He was mistaken.

Oscar began by telling Bonilla that he had recently become a Christian. The governor wanted to know what he meant by that.

'I was a person who, for 16 years, slept on the streets of Medellín in a drugged stupor,' Oscar explained. 'I was in and out of jail several times. By his grace, the Lord changed my life.

'After he finished transforming my life, God gave me a special call to preach the gospel to drug addicts and criminals like those here in Bellavista,' he added. 'I want to talk to the inmates about Christ.'

'That's fine,' Bonilla said. 'We will give you visiting privileges one hour a week. Tell me, what day do you want to come?'

Oscar set his jaw. 'One hour is not enough,' he said. 'I can't do anything in one hour a week. I want to come every day, all day. And I want permission to enter the cell blocks.'

Bonilla looked directly at Oscar. 'That is entirely out of the question, he said. 'We cannot guarantee your safety in the cell blocks.'

'I'm not worried about my safety,' Oscar countered. 'I have served time in this jail myself. I know what it's like.'

Bonilla blinked. This man with his honest face and neatly pressed white shirt was claiming that he had been a prisoner in Bellavista? The governor didn't believe it. Osorio did not fit the profile.

'You really expect me to believe that you were a prisoner in this jail?' Bonilla asked.

Oscar did not blink. 'Check your files, my name is there.'

'There's something else,' he added. 'The authorities still have a warrant out for my arrest on a burglary charge. You can look it up for yourself.'

Bonilla hesitated, then called his secretary and ordered her to search the prison files for one Oscar de Jesus Osorio. In a few minutes, she returned with a cardboard folder.

The governor opened the file and saw Oscar's photograph. His expression changed from scepticism to surprise. 'So, it is true,' he said. 'Now, would you like to tell me exactly what happened to you?'

Oscar sighed. 'I was a drug addict and criminal,' he repeated. 'God, by his grace, transformed me into the person you see before you. And I believe that just as Christ changed my life, he can change many lives in this prison.'

The governor sat still, pondering. What on earth motivated an ex-offender to return to prison as a volunteer preacher? Would Oscar really stick with it, or would he disappear after a few days? There was only one way to find out.

'Very well,' Bonilla said finally. He took out a piece of paper and jotted something down on it. A few days later, the prison staff presented Oscar Osorio with a pass. It authorized him to visit any cell block within Bellavista Jail on any day of the week for as many hours as he wished.

*   *   *

The special pass allowing him unlimited access to the cell blocks was about the only tangible asset Oscar Osorio had when he began working in the prison. Each morning, he and Carmenza prayed together before 7 o'clock when he said goodbye to her and boarded a bus for the commute to the prison. Carmenza left for her job at the telephone paging company, knowing she would not see her husband until evening.

Inmates gave the new evangelist a rude reception to Bellavista. Oscar learned to carry an extra shirt with him to the jail. Inmates pelted him with eggs, rotten food and bags of urine as he walked through the jail. Every evening he washed off the stench and changed into the clean shirt before leaving for home. *Caciques* watched to see if his activities would undermine their sovereignty over the prisoners. Inevitably, Oscar offended one or another of the prison potentates, who then threatened to kill him.

The problem was Oscar's message. One of his favourite texts of Scripture was Isaiah 61.1, 'The Spirit of the Lord God is upon me, because the Lord has anointed me to bring good tidings to the afflicted, he has sent me to bind up the broken-hearted, to proclaim liberty to the captives, and the opening of the prison to those who are bound.' Another was the account in Mark 5, of Jesus liberating the Gadarene man from a legion of abusive demons.

'Jesus wants to liberate you from the demons of drugs, crime and hatred,' Oscar announced in the patios. To ensure that the *carros* understood the significance of his message, the preacher would stand on the exact spot where they had recently committed a murder and amplify his words with a megaphone. The guilty glared at him and muttered gruesome descriptions of the fate that awaited him if he persisted with his preaching.

These were no idle threats. The rhythm of violence inside Bellavista had gained momentum since Oscar last spent time there. Battles between cell blocks had become a routine part of prison life. Daily body counts reached 3, 5, 10 or more. Corpses often laid in the corridors for hours before guards could collect them for burial.

Prison policy had changed to allow wives and girlfriends conjugal visits, so the incidence of homosexual rape had declined. Fights about rape had not. Wives and girlfriends were the trophies. Prisoners challenged husbands and boyfriends to hand-to-hand combat for their right to conjugal visits. If they refused to fight or lost the combat, rape ensued, sometimes in front of their eyes.

Prison guards had lost control over the prisoners. Many accepted bribes to look the other way, or to protect rapists and murderers from punishment. Rapists and murderers were punished with detention in'La Guayana', a row of cells on the top floor of the prison reserved for solitary confinement. However, due to overcrowding in Bellavista, the cells in La Guayana held four or five inmates each. There were no toilets there. Prisoners were allowed to leave the cramped cells for just one hour a day. A journalist who once visited La Guayana dubbed it the 'anteroom to hell'. Nobody wanted to go there.

Oscar Osorio went there. He visited La Guayana regularly, telling the prisoners that they were important to God and urging them to ask forgiveness for their sins. In response, they pelted the preacher with rubbish and bags of urine.

Oscar trusted God to protect him from those who threatened his life inside Bellavista. He could not depend on prison guards to protect him. Many of them cooperated with *caciques* to smuggle drugs and weapons into the prison. Some guards ended up as murder victims themselves.

One day after he finished preaching, Oscar was passing through a barred door with a group of prisoners. An officer named Zapata stood nearby, watching them exit. Suddenly an inmate grabbed Zapata by the hair, pulled a long blade from his trousers and began stabbing the officer repeatedly.'This is so you will keep your promises, you son of a b—h,' the killer screamed. Zapata crumpled to the ground, dead.

Officer Zapata had cooperated with the *caciques* to smuggle drugs and weapons into Bellavista. Oscar later learned he had fallen into disfavour because of an extortion scheme gone sour, so the *caciques* ordered him to be killed. Prison officials dispatched his assassin to La Guayana. The man spent the remaining years of his life in the anteroom to hell. But he saw Oscar Osorio there regularly, telling the prisoners that Jesus loved them.

*   *   *

Orlando Taborda also came to Bellavista prison. But unlike Oscar Osorio, the professional killer with the charismatic personality did not request entry.

I was working at the *sicario* business for five years when I got really desperate. In that world, one makes a lot of enemies. It's a world where you kill your best friend if someone offers you enough money.

I had separated from my wife. One day I telephoned her from Bogotá, where I had gone to do a job. She mentioned that a friend of mine – the same one who recruited me to work for the Mafia – had asked her for a date. This was a great insult. I left my staff in Bogotá to do the job and came back to Medellín to kill my friend. That night we committed an orgy, killing four people.

The following Sunday was Mother's Day. I was on my way to the shop to buy a present for my mama when a young fellow reached through the open car window at a traffic light and ripped off my Rayban sunglasses. I started hunting him. It wasn't so much the expensive glasses as the fact that he had stolen them from *me*, a *sicario*.

Six weeks later, somebody told me where the fellow was. Two of my employees said, 'Come on, let us kill him.' 'No,' I said, 'I will do it myself. After all, he offended the Boss.'

That afternoon about 4.30, I was waiting a block from a police station when I saw the fellow coming down the street. I had a pistol with a long silencer. I hit him with the first shot and he died. Just then, the police came up the street in an armed caravan, escorting a member of the city council. The bodyguards saw the weapon and thought I was going to assassinate the councilman. They all started shooting at me.

I started shooting back at them. One bullet hit me, passing through my liver. The police put me in their car and were going to finish me off, but I managed to speak up. I offered them money to let me go. They refused. They were about to shoot me in the head. I told them all kinds of things, until I finally convinced them not to kill me. They took me to a clinic. Half an hour after we arrived, a major from the police department came in. 'Why have you brought him in here?' he said. 'You were supposed to kill him.'

When I heard that, I started screaming. The doctor realized what was going on and refused to let them take me back outside.

They operated on me and sent me to Bellavista prison. The day I went there, I could sense the smell of death on the prison wagon. When you approached the jail, you could smell the death from outside. I spent the first month in the prison infirmary, along with other injured men. In that month, I saw 16 dead and 30 wounded. Even though I killed people, I was not capable of cutting them up like they did there. I saw corpses with a thousand knife wounds, with the heads cut off. It made a real impression on me.

I was sentenced to 22 years for possession of an illegal weapon and for malicious intent. After a month in the infirmary, they took me to Cell Block Eight. Since I was a *sicario*, a lot of people there knew me. I still carried a little money and started to butter up the *caciques* who ruled the cell block. If somebody came in and didn't get along with him, the *cacique* gave the order to have him killed. He had about 120 *carros* to carry out his orders. I started making friends with these fellows. I told the *caciques* that when the day came that they would be needing my services, I was here to help.

But I saw too many dead men. It was an incredibly violent prison. One day it hit me: Orlando, you are not going to last 22 years in here. My cousin Fernando came one Saturday to visit and I asked him to bring me some cyanide tablets. I wanted to commit suicide. He said to wait two weeks, perhaps someone would be able to get me out. If not, he would get me the cyanide.

*   *   *

In addition to the danger, jail ministry presented Oscar and Carmenza Osorio with another challenge: poverty. They had to keep living expenses at a minimum. Oscar ate breakfast and lunch each day at the prison mess hall to save on food bills at home. He mended his tattered shoes until they were beyond reconstruction. Shoes were important to Oscar because he sometimes walked home at night to save the bus fare.

But the sacrifices paid off. Within the first month of his arrival, Oscar could see tangible results.

The seeds first planted by the Rendle family, Mama Lilian, the Celis brothers and other Prison Fellowship volunteers were bearing fruit. A number of Bellavista inmates embraced the gospel. One of them was Adán Colorado, who was serving a sentence in Cell Block Four for car theft. It was the latest in a string of jail terms Colorado had served for armed robbery, drug-dealing and deadly assault over the previous 18 years.

Cell mates thought Colorado mad because he lived most of the time in a semiconscious stupor. The stupor, however, was *bazuco*-induced. Colorado bribed a prison guard to smuggle him a steady supply of the drug. Six months into his sentence, he suffered an attack of *bazuco*-induced *delirium tremens*. His ravings attracted the attention of prison guards, who thought Colorado genuinely mad and carried him off to the psychiatric ward.

Two days later, Colorado came to himself and saw he was living among 20 mad inmates. He commenced kicking the door of the psychiatric ward until he attracted the attention of the staff. He explained to them that he was not mad, but simply a casualty of too much *bazuco*. They returned him to Cell Block Four.

As he re-entered the cell block, Colorado saw some freshly painted words on the patio wall: 'Come to me, all who labour and are heavy laden, and I will give you rest.' The phrase fascinated him. Over the next few days, Colorado stood before the wall, contemplating the words. He did not know that they were from the Bible or that Jesus had spoken them. But they spoke to him profoundly. He asked around and located Horacio Morales, the inmate who had painted the text on the patio wall. Morales told Colorado that Jesus loved him and wanted to change his life. Adán began to weep. He fell to his knees under the words of Matthew 11.28 and there accepted Jesus.

Horacio introduced Adán to Luz Elena Torres, Javier Celis and other Prison Fellowship volunteers. They gave him a Bible and enrolled him in religion classes in the P3 educational centre. There he met Oscar Osorio, who conducted a brief worship service in P3 centre each morning between visits to the cell blocks. Oscar began paying daily visits to Adán, Horacio and four other inmates in Cell Block Four who had embraced the gospel. He taught them prayer, fasting and other basics of Christian discipleship.

Oscar also lent them his megaphone so that the new believers could preach to their fellow inmates in Cell Block Four. They responded by throwing bags of urine in the believers' faces and mocking. 'You are nothing but Pharisees and hypocrites,' they sneered. 'Stop that preaching or they will be carrying your corpses out of here.'

The believers kept preaching and the mockery kept building. Fellow prisoners stole the believers' Bibles and tore out the pages. They did not do this purely out of malice. Drug users had discovered that the fine paper used in Bibles was especially good for rolling *bazuco* cigarettes. The believers told Oscar of the thefts and showed him their damaged Bibles. He responded by tearing out more pages, writing 'Jesus loves you' on them, and slipping them under doors on his rounds through the jail.

One day Adán told Oscar that a gang of 30 *carros* were plotting an assault on the small group of believers. What should they do? 'There is nothing we can do but keep still and wait for God to glorify himself,' Oscar said. The seven men spent the day together fasting and praying in Colorado's tiny cubicle, aware that the following day the 30 *carros* would attack them.

However, a bloody fight broke out among the *carros* themselves the next morning. Every one of the 30 fell wounded in the mêlée; four of them died. Colorado watched guards remove one victim to the infirmary, a long blade sticking clean through his body. A phrase he had learned from Psalm 91 suddenly came to mind: 'My eyes have seen the downfall of my enemies, my ears have heard the doom of my evil assailants.' Adán knew

God had used extreme measures to protect the small band of believers in Cell Block Four. But he was sorry for the wounded man nonetheless.

Miraculously, medics in the prison infirmary were able to save the *carro's* life. After his recovery, prison officials ordered him to be confined to La Guayana, where he received regular visits from Oscar Osorio. Eventually, he too embraced the gospel.

Interest in the gospel mushroomed in Cell Block Four after the unsuccessful assault on the believers. Every morning at 6.30, Adán and Horacio gathered the group to sing hymns and hear gospel preaching. Oscar taught them prayer, fasting and other basics of Christian discipleship. More prisoners prayed the prayer of faith, surrendering weapons in exchange for Bibles. Over the next six months, the band of believers increased from six to 80. At that point, Oscar decided it was time to pay another call on Governor Bonilla.

Fernando Bonilla looked across his desk at the man with his honest face and neatly pressed white shirt. Oscar Osorio gazed steadily back at the governor.

'Let me get this straight,' the governor said. 'You are telling me that you can no longer meet in the classrooms we have provided for you because they are too small. What do you want me to do?'

Oscar leaned forward in his chair. 'I want you to give me permission to repair the Protestant chapel here in Bellavista.'

'Out of the question,' Bonilla said. 'I have no budget to do that.'

'I'm not asking for a budget, I'm only asking for permission.'

'Who will pay for it?'

'The Lord.'

The governor wanted to know what he meant by that. After all, the Lord would need a hefty budget for chapel reconstruction. The building had fallen into neglect since the Rendles moved from Medellín to Bogotá several years before. Inmates shattered the windows and defaced the walls. They pilfered wood from floors, ceilings and pews to build partitions in the cell blocks. The roof would have to be repaired, as well as the plumbing and electrical wiring.

Oscar explained to the governor that some of the prisoners had offered contributions to the project out of their own pockets and agreed to do all the work. He had not yet asked the evangelical churches in Medellín for donations, he said, but was confident that some of them would help with the expenses. Oscar knew the building trade and would supervise the project himself.

Bonilla listened quietly to Osorio's idea. He had no doubts about the man's ability to pull off the restoration project. However, he did see a potential problem: the prison's Roman Catholic chaplain. Catholicism was the state religion of Colombia. The constitution did not allow other faiths to function openly in public institutions. If the priest objected to the plan and pressed the issue with Bonilla's superiors in INPEC, the National Institute of Prisons, the governor would have a lot of explaining to do.

He looked across his desk again at Oscar, who gazed steadily back at Bonilla. The governor realized he could do the politically correct thing and deny the request, or he could do the right thing. Bonilla decided to do the right thing. He took out a paper and jotted something down on it. Oscar Osorio had permission to renovate the chapel.

That evening he took Governor Bonilla's letter to Gwyn Lewis, a missionary of the Covenant Evangelical Church and a Prison Fellowship volunteer. Lewis called a friend in North America who he thought might be able to help. A few days later, a cheque for $2,000 arrived for building materials. Oscar suspended his preaching in the cell blocks for two months to supervise inmates working on the repairs. Bellavista's Roman Catholic chaplain did learn of the project and registered objections, but did not halt the work. The Protestant chapel re-opened for worship. At the inaugural service, Oscar baptized 30 believers in a makeshift baptistery. The Lord was indeed building his church inside Bellavista.

*   *   *

'I did not believe in anything of any kind. I didn't even believe in myself. The world, humankind, these things did not matter to me at all. Every day, one of my cell mates, Alvaro Roldan, would say to me, "Jesus loves you," and I would answer him with the choicest vulgarities I could think of.'

Gerardo 'Papa' Pino was still defending himself with the foulest mouth in Bellavista. But his disagreeable manners and searing profanity did him no good at all.

Alvaro attended the chapel services. He was an invalid, so the believers carried him there on their backs. One day, they sent word to me saying, 'Alvaro needs you in the cell.' I said, 'Why would that cripple call me? I don't need him for anything.' I went and stuck my head in the cell and he says to me, 'Pino, the brothers went and left me here.' I said, 'Man, there are 800 fellows in this cell block and you come to me, a man you consider a devil?' He said, 'Pino just do me this one favour. Don't leave me here.'

So I picked him up and went out. In the patio, everybody saw me carrying him on my back and started heckling. 'Look here, Pino is going to visit the evangelicals!' I took Alvaro to the chapel and set him down. He caught my shirt tail and said, 'Luz Elena Torres needs to talk to you.' I said, 'What does that old woman want with me?'

At that instant, I heard the metal door close. All the inmates had arrived in the chapel from the cell blocks, so the guard had locked us in. I was forced to stay until the service ended. I spewed out the ugliest words I could think of.

The worship began. It seemed as if my head exploded. I could not bear listening to the songs. Afterwards, Oscar Osorio preached. I presumed the whole message was aimed right at me. I was quite offended. That night Alvaro came to me and said, 'Jesus loves you. What a blessing it was that you were in the service today!' I tried to swear at him, but couldn't get the words out.

The next day just before noon, Pastor Oscar showed up at the cell block gate and had them call me. Seeing it was

him, I said, 'So, it's you! What do you want with me?' He
said, 'Listen, we have to talk. They let me out to talk to him.
He put his arm around me and started talking until he had
me in the chapel office. I didn't realize where I was until I
heard the door slam. They trapped me in the chapel again.

Suddenly everybody was saying to me, 'Papa Pino, here
again? What a blessing! Isn't the work of God marvellous!'
I felt something odd within me when they started the
songs. I eventually loosened up and started clapping my
hands. Oscar smiled at me and I thought to myself, this
fellow cares about the likes of even me. He preached on
Psalm 91. It was wonderful. When he finished he said, 'How
many of you want to confess Jesus as your Saviour?' Six
men went down to the front. I tried to leave my seat but
could not take the first step. Somebody was pulling me
from behind. I looked around, but nobody was there. I
lunged, got myself moving and went down front with the
other six. Oscar began praying for us.

I felt a wind blowing against my whole body. I said to
myself, this is really strange. Oscar put his hand on my
head and said I should repeat after him. When I started
praying, I felt like I was rising upward, floating in the air,
light as a feather, with my eyes closed. How in the world
am I going to get down from here, I thought. When he
finished, I opened my eyes and everything was fine.

Oscar gave me a Bible. 'How can I take this, I don't know
how to read?' I said. 'Take it, you deserve it,' he said. So I
took it back to the cell block. Boy, what a teasing I got from
the fellows there. 'Look here, Papa Pino got religion! See
how they brainwashed him!' I said nothing, kept my head
bowed and went to the cell to caress my Bible.

I had not learned a thing about reading in school, but
that night I started putting words together. From one
moment to the next, I was actually reading the Bible and
it was registering in my head. I started attending chapel
every day. A week later, Luz Elena Torres said to me: 'Come,
I am going to give you some verses to memorize. They
present the plan of salvation.' I said, 'I still can't read very

well.' 'The Holy Spirit will give you the ability,' she said. 'The Scriptures say that we all have the mind of Christ.'

She gave me three verses, Romans 3.23, 5.8 and 6.23. The next week, I went back and recited them to her. She wrote out three more: Romans 8.1, 8.16–17 and 8.29. I recited those three and Elena hugged me. 'My good Pino, look how well it's going for you!' she said. She taught me 23 Bible verses dealing with the plan of salvation. Ever since, I've had them stored here in my head, all 23.

*   *   *

Across town from Bellavista Prison, and high on a hill ventilated by spring-like breezes from the Aburra Valley, sits the tidy campus of the Biblical Seminary of Colombia. Founded in the 1940s by OMS Mission, the school attracts students from many Latin American countries, despite being located in the continent's most dangerous city.

Jeannine Brabon spent her childhood in Medellín, her parents being of the missionary generation that founded the Biblical Seminary. Harold and Margaret Brabon raised their four children in the midst of *La Violencia*. Jeannine learned firsthand the risks of living in Colombia. As a girl of 11, she heard the voice of God calling her to follow in her parents' footsteps. 'But I can't be a missionary,' she told him. 'I'm not brave enough.'

After completing university training in the USA, Jeannine accepted a missionary assignment in Madrid, working with teenagers and doing book-keeping for the OMS Spanish office. But the young woman could not get Colombia out of her system. Her father once wrote her a letter about the urgent needs in Colombia. 'Time is running out,' he told her. 'Act while it is day.' Four days later, Harold Brabon died unexpectedly of a heart attack.

Following her father's counsel, Jeannine began commuting annually from Spain to Medellín to teach short courses at the Biblical Seminary. She discovered urgent needs among the students, counselling young women who suffered rape and sexual abuse, comforting young men whose fathers and brothers died in guerrilla warfare. One student told of a conversation he had with a neighbour. The man remarked that he was on his way to commit murder. He had nothing against the victim, he said, he simply needed the money to put food on the table. The student convinced him at that moment to embrace the gospel and thus helped save two lives.

Mark Wittig, who also grew up in Medellín as a child of OMS missionaries, returned as an adult to teach at the Biblical Seminary. An avid athlete, Mark founded a football school for boys from the city slums. One of his early recruits, Wilson Rojas, became a Christian and later a coach. One day on the playing field, Wilson snatched an Uzi sub-machine gun away from a 12-year-old who tried to use it to settle a dispute with an opposing player. Wilson convinced the boys to resolve their conflict on biblical principle instead, and thus helped save two more lives.

One day in September 1987, Jeannine was walking across the campus of the Biblical Seminary thinking about the urgent needs in Colombia. In a few days she would return to Madrid to resume her duties in the OMS Spanish office. She said to herself: If only I had more time here, I could do more. At that instant she heard a voice, clear as a bell, answer: 'When you come here to live permanently, you will.'

Jeannine knew it was the voice of God when, the next day, Theo Donner, vice-rector of the Biblical Seminary, asked if he could present her name to the board of directors as a candidate for the permanent faculty. The school had never placed a woman on its permanent faculty, so Jeannine felt safe that her chances of being selected were nil. She was mistaken. The same week, the board voted unanimously to employ her to teach Hebrew and serve as dean of women. Upon her return to Spain, Jeannine announced her intention to move permanently to Medellín.

Other American missionaries in Medellín were likewise moving – out of the city. The latest round in the drug war had claimed the lives of too many innocent bystanders. Almost everyone in the expatriate community knew of someone – the cook's husband, a boy on their son's football team, a local bus driver – who had died in the escalating violence. Some were casualties of frequent car bombings, others fell in drive-by shootings. In a few cases, victims simply disappeared, snatched from the street on the way to work or abducted from home in the middle of the night.

Foreign organizations began ordering their employees home. The Covenant Evangelical Mission recalled Gwyn Lewis and the Celis brothers. Other missions ordered their personnel to move to the relative safety of Bogotá. By late 1989, the staff of the Biblical Seminary were the only expatriate missionaries remaining in Medellín. OMS leaders asked them to consider evacuation as well. The small group discussed the option, but felt they could abandon neither their work nor their Colombian colleagues. It was a tough decision, but once it was made an unusual peace settled over the tidy campus on the hill overlooking Medellín.

*   *   *

'A week after my cousin's visit, I was desperate, I couldn't wait any longer. I wanted to take my life right then.'

Inside Bellavista, Orlando Taborda decided it was time to die. Being a religious man, he knew the importance of paying his respects to the Almighty before following through on the decision.

I went to see Juan Carlos Corredor, a man who read the Bible. I said, 'Carlos, I am going to commit suicide. I can't spend 22 years in this jail. He began talking to me about Jesus Christ. I said: 'Look, I'm very religious. I cross myself three or four times before killing a man. When I shipped drugs to Italy, I lit candles before the Virgin of the Sabaneta, asking her to help me get the merchandise through.'

He said: 'I'm going to talk to you about Jesus Christ. He wants to give you a life, not a religion.'

He started telling me about the love of Jesus. Neither my father nor mother loved me, they had no time for me. Once I was an adult, I bought love from women. I gave lots of gifts to my friends so that they would say I was their friend.

I had never known love for free. But this fellow tells me that Jesus Christ loved me so much that he gave his life for me. That made quite an impression on me.

Corredor gave me a Bible and I began reading it. Soon after that, two cell blocks went to war. The *caciques* called me over and said, 'Orlando, we need you to fight.' They took out all the weapons they had – hundreds of knives, pistols and grenades – and went around giving one to each of the inmates. I got my weapon, went down to the patio and put on a bandanna. The war cry sounded.

I had started reading the Bible and the words stuck in my mind. The words were saying to me, 'God is looking down upon this.' So I said, 'Well, God, I know you won't get angry if I only kill those who come at me.' The men from the other cell block were trying to come in. One of our fellows threw a grenade in the middle of them and the fighting began. There were 52 wounded, and three dead. The police arrived and there was shooting all over. I ducked into the cell and found Juan Carlos. I said, 'Is it right for me to have this weapon in my hand? I read in the Bible that, if your enemy strikes you on the right cheek, you should turn the left cheek.'

In that moment, I felt something like the presence of God. I went to the *cacique* and said to him: 'Do you know what? I am not going to fight anymore. I am going to kneel before God.' I handed the knife back to him.

Later Juan Carlos said to me: 'Look, Orlando, you ought to go out to the chapel. There is an evangelical chaplain there, they call him Brother Oscar. He can give you better guidance.'

5

Riot and Revival

Mery Perez had barely spoken to Carmenza and Oscar since their wedding day. But in May 1987, she began to spend time daily at the modest apartment where her daughter and son-in-law lived. The reason was her new granddaughter, Juliana.

Juliana's birth accomplished a reconciliation between Carmenza and her family. But the baby's arrival presented another dilemma for her mother. Carmenza was still the sole bread-winner in the Osorio household and could not interrupt her career to stay at home with Juliana. Mery Perez solved the problem, volunteering to care for her granddaughter so Carmenza could continue working. When her maternity leave expired, she returned to her position at the telephone paging service.

Eventually, her career presented a dilemma for Carmenza as well. She learned that some of her company's clients worked for the Medellín drug cartel. Drug enforcement agents traced traffickers' calls to the paging service. Police staged several raids on the office where Carmenza worked, confiscating communications equipment and escorting employees to headquarters for questioning. The constant interference made it difficult for Carmenza to do her job, and the suspicion of ties between her company and the cartel placed her at risk of arrest.

'The problem is Pablo Escobar,' she told Oscar one evening after dinner. 'He has so much money and influence in this town, that the police think anyone with a pager works for him.'

'I don't feel right about working there,' she added. 'For a Christian to be involved in these things is just not proper.'

'There really is only one solution,' Oscar told her.

'What's that?'

'You must resign.'

'I think it's best,' she agreed. 'But how will we live?'

'The Lord will provide,' Oscar said.

Oscar thought perhaps the Lord's provision might come in the form of a new job for Carmenza or one for himself, but God had another idea. Gwyn Lewis had been in touch with more of his friends. A few days after Carmenza stopped working, he telephoned Oscar to say that he had raised enough money to provide a salary for Oscar to work in the prison ministry.

The support from family and friends could not have come at a better time for Oscar and Carmenza. The rising wealth and influence of Pablo Escobar would make life even more difficult and dangerous for them.

*   *   *

Before his death in 1993 at the age of 44, Pablo Escobar had sent more of his countrymen to their graves than any Colombian in recent history.

While still a teenager, he launched his criminal career stealing tombstones. Later, he joined a band of *sicarios* and turned to kidnap and murder. In 1975, Escobar smuggled his first kilo of cocaine into the United States, earning a $40,000 profit. With the money, he founded the Medellín drug cartel, which grew into a multimillion-dollar business within two years.

Escobar had not completed high school and fancied himself a Colombian Horatio Alger, a rags-to-riches business hero who could pull his country up from Third World poverty to a first-class economic power. The trouble was, Escobar's business was illegal. For years, the Medellín cartel lobbied the government to legalize cocaine, mounting a sophisticated public relations campaign to promote the medicinal benefits of the drug. When the tactic failed, Escobar turned to bribery and murder. The choice between 'silver or lead' – accept our money or take a bullet – confronted police officers, district attorneys, judges and any other public servant who interfered with the cartel's multimillion-dollar business.

Some of those public servants worked inside Bellavista. As the drug war escalated in the late 1980s, Escobar began taking a personal interest in the jail. Because several of his business associates were incarcerated there, Escobar used his considerable resources to organize escapes. One daring break-out employed a helicopter, which landed in the prison yard in broad daylight and extracted six inmates. Embarrassed INPEC officials suspected that the cartel must have bribed members of the prison staff to cooperate with the escape, but they did not know which ones. So they fired some and reassigned others, including top administrators. The cartel knew exactly which members of the prison staff had refused to cooperate, so they threatened some and murdered others, including top administrators.

Pablo Escobar's determination to liberate his associates from Bellavista and INPEC officials' determination to keep them there translated into escalating violence. The cartel organized a mass escape in May 1989. This time INPEC officials learned of the attempt and reinforced the Bellavista guards with police sharpshooters. In the ensuing gunfight, two officers and 15 inmates died, according to Medellín press reports. The Medellín press, however, did not always report accurate body counts. Prison officials sometimes withheld information from journalists for security reasons. Pablo Escobar sometimes convinced journalists to distort the information they did gather, by offering them the choice between silver or lead.

Anyone who lived or worked inside Bellavista knew for a fact that the body count was rising dramatically. Prison guards who refused to cooperate with the cartel suffered heavy casualties. Assassins stabbed officers to death in prison corridors. Masked gunmen forced them off city buses while on their way home from work and shot them dead before the eyes of fellow passengers. Gunmen broke into guards' homes and shot them dead before the eyes of their families. In some cases, they shot the families dead before the eyes of the guards.

Prison staff, including top administrators, tried to escape the violence by transferring to other prisons, such as La Picota in Bogotá. But Escobar had associates there, too, and arranged the assassination of prison staff, including top administrators.

Prison staff, of course, were not the only casualties. Escobar instructed his *sicarios* to eliminate inmates who worked for the rival Cali cartel, as well as those who refused to work for his own organization. Assassins inflicted the harshest executions on anyone suspected of being a *sapo*. *Sapos* were informants who cooperated with prison officials, passing along information about the cartel and its escape plans.

The cartel suspected an inmate named Oscar Taborda of being a *sapo*. One day Taborda was standing in the patio of his cell block when a *sicario* came up and shot him twice in the head. Other inmates pounced on the fallen man and riddled his dead body with knife wounds. Taborda's brutal assassination was similar to scores of others inside Bellavista, except that it took place on a Saturday, during visiting hours, before the eyes of his own son.

Murders sparked retaliation, which led to more murders. One afternoon, a business associate of Pablo Escobar was playing football in the athletic yard when another inmate pulled a pistol from his trousers and shot him dead. The brazen murder required vengeance, especially in light of the fact that the dead man was a *cacique*. His *carros* concluded that the assassin must have bribed a prison guard to smuggle the weapon through the door, but they did not know which one. So they decided to kill every guard on duty the day of the murder.

Two days later, Oscar Osorio was leaving Bellavista at 6 p.m. for home. As he said goodbye to the guards at the main gate, he noticed the tension in their faces. The plan of revenge had begun to claim victims. No one knew who would be next. The shift captain was going off duty and greeted Oscar, who was waiting for a bus to take him home.

Two men came along the road on a motorcycle. As they reached Bellavista's main gate, one pulled a sub-machine gun from his coat. Oscar heard a brief burst of gunfire, tat-tat-tat, and saw the captain fall dead. The motorcycle sped out of sight around the corner.

That night after dinner, Oscar told Carmenza of the murder and the escalating violence inside Bellavista.

'There really is only one solution,' she said.

'What's that?'

'The Lord,' Carmenza said. 'He is the only one who can bring peace to the jail.'

Despite the rising body count, Carmenza never once entertained the idea of asking Oscar to withdraw from the prison ministry. After all, it was what her husband was meant to do and she would support him in it, however the Lord directed her.

Bellavista, January 1990

'I went to talk with Brother Oscar Osorio. He spoke to me more completely about the Lord Jesus and invited me to pray the prayer of faith. I felt something marvellous that day. There were no words to express it.'

Orlando Taborda, con man, wife beater and *sicario*, found Jesus in Bellavista Prison.

I returned to the cell block very happy. It bothered me, though, to meet with the believers, because the other inmates didn't treat them well at all. I was very vain. One day the pastor read in the Bible where it says, 'For whoever is ashamed of me and my words in this adulterous and sinful generation, of him will the Son of Man also be ashamed, when he comes in the glory of his Father with the holy angels.' That verse had an impact on me and I started to meet with the brothers in the cell block.

So, it was my turn to get bathed with urine. I prayed for several days, that I would not get angry. I kept meeting with the brothers and God began to give me words to speak to the *caciques*. I said to one: 'Brother, you know the life I used to lead. It didn't work. Now look at the life God is giving. You can't buy this with all the money you might get hold of in this world. You can laugh. I used to laugh with my lips, but my heart was crying. You know yourself that, at night, we all cry in that cell. But now I laugh in my heart, because God is so marvellous.'

After a month walking in the gospel, the fellow that had been preaching in our cell block was transferred. Several of the brothers said, 'Orlando, why don't you preach?' I prayed and fasted and asked God to give me the words. The next day God gave me a message. I would never have been able to preach it on my own.

I started to fast, to pray a lot. I tried to show the gospel for what it is: a life. Every morning, the fellows would stand before an image in the cell block, repeat the Ave Maria and cross themselves. But with the same hands, they killed and stole and dealt drugs. I started to talk to them about everything God required. Two weeks later, about 70 people were meeting with us. Brother Oscar would teach me in the chapel and I would go and preach in the cell block. I just put myself in God's hands.

In that same month, word came that they had reduced my sentence by ten years. I would only have to serve 12 years behind bars. They started saying to me, 'Pistolero, you think the Bible is going to do your time for you?' I said, 'No, not the Bible. But God says in Isaiah 61.1 that he came to proclaim liberty to the captives and the opening of the prison to those who are bound.'

I prayed to God that he would not take me out until he saw that I could be a true servant of his. I could serve a 12-year prison term with Christ, but I could not be on the street even one day without him.

*   *   *

By the beginning of 1990, violence against prison guards had reached intolerable levels. The officers held counsel and voted to go on strike. None wished to risk their lives anymore inside the killing ground that Bellavista had become. Guards locked the gates and refused to allow anyone inside, not even the new governor, Hader Ramirez. Instead, they presented him with a list of demands, urging Ramirez to call in the Colombian army to restore order. Meanwhile, officers picketed outside the walls and distributed leaflets to passing motorists. The handbills described the violence inside Bellavista and asked the public to support the guards' demand for a military takeover.

News of the strike drew Medellín's press corps to the gates of Bellavista. Reports of the carnage were aired on TV and filled the newspapers. Each day journalists reported the latest body count: 8, 13, 22. The numbers represented a count-down to the military action that everyone expected would come. When it did, it would leave in its wake the largest body count Bellavista had ever seen.

When inmates learned of the officers' protest, the jail exploded in violence. Entire cell blocks went to war as *caciques* tried to exert their will over the unsupervised prison. They unleashed their *carros* to settle old scores against enemy *caciques*. *Sicarios* attacked each other with renewed ferocity.

Corpses littered the patios and corridors of Bellavista. Murderers cut off arms and legs, gouged out eyes. They used the blood of their victims to sketch weapons and skeletons on prison walls and to write obscene graffiti ridiculing *sapos* and rival gangs. Prison officials had lost control of the jail. Pablo Escobar had instigated the terror, but could not halt it. Even the *caciques* were helpless to stop the slaughter, once it commenced. Bellavista obeyed but one lord. Death was his name.

*   *   *

One morning at his usual hour, Oscar Osorio arrived at the main gate of Bellavista and discovered he could not enter the prison. Guards told him they were on strike and pushed a leaflet into his hand. The preacher read the handbill and realized that Bellavista was approaching a calamity of unprecedented proportions. This called for extraordinary measures.

He invited other Prison Fellowship volunteers to join him on a bluff overlooking the jail for prayer and fasting. A group of older women accepted. On the sixth day of the fast, Oscar saw a vision from the bluff. An enormous hand reached down and cradled Bellavista in its palm. Oscar, weakened by the fast, thought he was hallucinating. But with the vision came a voice, clear as a bell. 'Organize an evangelistic campaign inside Bellavista,' it said. 'Bring singers and preachers and amplifiers. Play the national anthem and ask the prisoners to raise white flags.'

The vision vanished. Oscar was looking once again upon Bellavista. He heard the tat-tat-tat of gunfire and the screams of wounded and dying men. But he could not deny he had seen the hand of God and heard his voice.

*　　*　　*

Oscar Osorio sat across the desk of Hader Ramirez, governor of Bellavista Jail. He had come to ask a favour. Governor Ramirez knew it was not going to be a small favour.

'I believe the Lord Jesus Christ is going to change Bellavista,' Oscar told him. 'He is going to stop the violence.'

Ramirez wanted to know what Oscar meant by that.

'We want to hold a campaign in the jail. We want to have music, preachers, amplifiers.'

'God gave me a vision to make white flags,' Oscar continued, his voice urgent. 'We are going to give one to every inmate. You must play the national anthem over the loudspeakers in the whole prison. We Christians will ask each inmate to raise his white flag and pray to the Lord.'

Ramirez blinked. This is it, he thought. The violence here has driven even Oscar Osorio mad. He peered intently into the preacher's eyes to detect some sign of mental disturbance. Oscar returned his steady gaze.

'Let me get this straight,' the governor said with some hesitation. 'My officers tell me it's too dangerous for them to set foot inside the cell blocks. The inmates are going berserk. The press and the public are urging me to call up the army. In the midst of all this, God told you we are going to stop the rioting with white flags?'

'That's right,' Oscar replied, his voice still urgent. 'Christians have been fasting and praying for this prison for months now. Over four hundred inmates are attending our meetings. Of those, 120 have been baptized. We believe God is ready to do something here.'

For several moments, the governor sat thinking. Osorio's plan was undoubtedly the most absurd strategy to quell a prison riot in the history of law enforcement. What would his superiors in INPEC think of Ramirez if he went along with the scheme? Perhaps that he, too, had finally gone mad. What if Osorio's plan failed? Ramirez would become the laughing-stock of the national prison system. On the other hand, what if Osorio's plan worked . . . ?

'Okay,' Ramirez said, 'you may do what you may do.'

That night, Oscar called Jairo Chalarca and told him about the campaign he was organizing for Bellavista. Oscar asked Pastor Chalarca to preach. He agreed. Also, Oscar said, he would like the singing group from the Covenant Evangelical Church to come and bring their sound equipment. Chalarca agreed to that, as well. After dinner that evening, Oscar and Carmenza began cutting white paper into triangles and pasting them onto plastic straws. The following Sunday, Osorio arrived at Bellavista with Jairo Chalarca, the Covenant Evangelical Church singers and thousands of tiny white flags.

*   *   *

'At one time in '89, I witnessed the deaths of 13 persons, then of eight more. The *caciques* were the reason for the homicides. They made war on each other.'

In his cell block inside Bellavista, Papa Pino watched the violence escalate. Then, it suddenly ceased.

They abducted two guards and they were found dead in the cell block. The law of silence ruled, so no one said anything. The jail shut down for days. There were lots of problems. There were over 4,000 men in the jail, but there was room for only 1,500. It was too much.

Then I became involved in the white flag campaign. Brother Oscar and the other preachers he brought went through every cell block, preaching the message. They used amplifiers. Women also helped preach the Word. We marched along singing: 'The walls are falling, the walls are falling, and the chains are being broken.'

It was a formidable witness. Many were converted in the campaign. The deaths started dwindling, until there was not one single casualty. Many surrendered their blades and pistols. One day, a whole group of prisoners handed over their weapons to Oscar himself. It was quite marvellous.

On the day he initiated his evangelistic campaign, Oscar Osorio passed out white flags to every inmate in Bellavista. While Christian prisoners prayed, the strains of the national anthem boomed out over the prison's loudspeakers:

> The horrible night has ended,
> Sublime liberty sheds the aurora
> Of her invincible light.
> The whole of humanity, groaning in chains,
> Comprehends the words of he
> Who died on the cross.
>
> Oh! unfading glory!
> Oh! immortal jubilee!
> From furrows of sorrow
> Goodness now springs.

The music faded. Oscar Osorio's voice came across the loudspeakers. He asked every inmate to raise his white flag and bow his head. Oscar began to pray. 'Lord Jesus, we ask you to forgive us. Forgive us for shedding so much blood. Forgive our kidnappings, our homicides, every one of our crimes.'

During that prayer, the smell of death hanging over Bellavista began to evaporate. Prisoners laid down blood-stained blades and ice picks. Some prayed the prayer of faith on the spot, repeating the words that came over the loud-speakers.

Every day for the next two months, Osorio, Jairo Chalarca, the musicians from the Covenant Evangelical Church and other Prison Fellowship volunteers marched through Bellavista singing, preaching and raising white flags. In the cell blocks, Orlando Taborda, Papa Pino and other Christian prisoners fasted, prayed and raised white flags. Oscar led prayers for the sick, for the repentant. He anointed with oil the sites where dead bodies had once lain and prayed for reconciliation. He anointed walls covered with blood-red graffiti and dark, satanic symbols and prayed for cleansing.

During the two months of the campaign a remarkable thing happened. The killing in Bellavista stopped. Guards reported no deaths, no wounded. A puzzled Hader Ramirez summoned Oscar to his office to find out what had happened. 'Don't worry, Governor sir,' Oscar said, 'God has taken the prison in his hand.' He showed Ramirez a burlap bag full of bloodied blades and ice picks that inmates had surrendered to him. 'They told me they want no more war,' he said.

Bellavista's body count dropped to zero. Oscar's absurd strategy for quelling the riots worked. Truthfully, he had seen the hand of God and heard his voice.

*   *   *

In Cell Block Eight, Orlando Taborda witnessed firsthand the impact the white flag campaign produced on Bellavista.

There was a lot of violence in those days in the cell block. The *caciques' carros* cut up the victims. They chopped one man in pieces, put the pieces in plastic bags and threw them in the trash can. They cut another man's head off, stuck his member in the mouth, and played football with it.

We believers in the cell block were meeting every morning from 6 to 7 o'clock to pray. We met again from 6 to 9 p.m. to study the Word of God. That's when Brother Oscar told me. 'Orlando, God gave me a vision and I feel we must have a campaign in the cell blocks.' We asked permission of the *caciques* and they said, yes, we could preach.

We had everything planned to begin on the wives' visiting day. The Thursday before, a war broke out between gangs of blacks and whites. There were 16 wounded, three dead. They cut one fellow in half. We thought perhaps the campaign would be cancelled. But we kept praying and fasting, and on Sunday we went through the cell block. We started on the third floor, praying in every corridor and stairway until we reached the ground floor. We finished with singing and prayers for the sick. That day a lot of men received Christ.

From exactly that date, I spent 18 more months in that cell block, and there was not so much as one injury. Everybody was saying, 'Something strange has happened here. We aren't evangelicals, but those people prayed and we feel something strange here, like peace and joy.' We knew it was the presence of God. People said, 'Even though I don't believe in God, what he does is real.'

The *caciques* issued an order that no one could touch us Christians, nor soak us with urine, nor insult us, nor steal our Bibles. The doors began to open to preach the gospel in all the cell blocks. We went into every one.

Medellín's press corps grew more and more sceptical about the events inside Bellavista Jail. For several days, they had come to the gates to gather information on the latest body count. 'How many new casualties?' they asked. 'None,' the guards replied. The reporters concluded that Governor Ramirez had authorized the army to quell the violence. They suspected the military of staging a secretive, night-time strike that had ended in a bloody massacre. The press smelled a cover-up. They insisted that Governor Ramirez allow them entry to the prison. The journalists expected to find mass graves full of fresh corpses. They were prepared to report the grisly truth.

They were not prepared for what they actually found inside Bellavista. Crowds of prisoners gathered in the cell blocks and patios were singing hymns, praying fervently and listening to evangelical preachers expound Bible messages.

*   *   *

In Cell Block Eight, Orlando Taborda witnessed firsthand the scepticism of Medellín journalists investigating the riots.

The press was coming daily to Bellavista to investigate how many dead and wounded there were. The officers began to say, 'There are none, not even one.' Pretty soon the reporters thought they were covering up the truth. So, they insisted on entering the cell blocks themselves.

There they saw big groups of Christians. We would meet in the patios at 6 in the morning. We would leave for the chapel, the pastor would preach and share the Word with us, then we'd go back to the cell block and meet some more. The reporters were quite impressed because Bellavista had not suffered a single casualty in some time.

When they asked us why, we said, 'Look, Bellavista has a new *cacique*, the Lord Jesus Christ. He has taken over this jail. That's what you're seeing here.' So they published the news of what was happening and told how the Lord was at work.

*   *   *

Governor Hader Ramirez was also quite impressed with the work the Lord Jesus had done in Bellavista. Several months had passed after the white flag campaign and the prison was still at peace. On 4 July 1990, Ramirez wrote a letter to Dr Joaquin Castro, president of Prison Fellowship of Colombia.

Doctor Joaquin Castro,

Receive my cordial greeting:

It is with joy that we can communicate the achievements which we have experienced, thanks in large part to all of you. As is now public knowledge, the situation in which this establishment lived was critical, everywhere ANARCHY and DISORDER [*sic*] reigned. Nevertheless, with the help of God and through all of you, we have been able to transform the situation to the point that today the deaths, disturbances and escape attempts have been reduced significantly.

Without doubt, it has been demonstrated once again that the labour you carry out on behalf of the inmates constitutes the finest assistance and collaboration on which the governors of our penal centres can depend.

We hope to continue receiving your valuable collaboration. Certainly the labour you are performing in this Antioquia jail is a blessing of God.

Yours attentively,
Hader Ramirez Barragan
Governor

Oscar Osorio had proved an effective peacemaker, but the danger to his own life still existed. One day he was preaching in the patio of Cell Block Four when a *cacique* came up to him with a pistol.

He forced Oscar into his cell and said, 'I am going to kill you, preacher. I'm going to take your life right now, so you won't come around here anymore.'

'You are ruining my drug business, preacher,' the *cacique* said. 'Nobody buys drugs from me now. They're all taking up that Bible.'

The *cacique* put the gun to Oscar's head. At that moment, God gave the preacher words to speak to his intended killer. He looked the *cacique* directly in the eye.

'If God gave you permission to harm me, you may. But if God did not give you permission, you cannot lay a finger on me.'

The man's jaw dropped open as if Oscar had struck him in the face. Saying nothing, he lowered the gun and opened the cell door. Oscar left and went back to preaching to the little congregation seated on the concrete floor of the patio.

A few days later, Oscar walked through Bellavista's corridors surveying the graffiti scrawled in blood on the prison walls. The white flag campaign had stopped the killing, but reminders of the jail's violent past remained. Oscar knew that the grisly images of guns, skeletons and obscenities could only have an unhealthy impact on the collective psychology of Bellavista's inmates. The figures could even inspire another outbreak of rioting. While he pondered this, God gave him another vision.

Oscar went to see Hader Ramirez. 'God told me to repaint the prison – patios, cell blocks, corridors, everything,' he told the governor.

'We don't have any budget to repaint the jail,' Ramirez said.

'But it must be done. Everywhere you look there are blood sketches of pistols, knives and skulls. You read nothing but profanity and scorn. The walls of some cells are painted entirely black and decorated with satanic symbols.'

'Where will you get the paint?'

'The Lord.'

Ramirez sighed. 'It's okay with me if you want to try this, but first you must talk to the *caciques*. See what they think.'

Oscar polled the *caciques* in each of the cell blocks. They listened to his proposal and said it was fine. Whatever Oscar wanted to do, he could go ahead and do it. Make yourself at home, they said. The *caciques* would see that the inmates cooperated fully with the plan.

Having surmounted that hurdle, Oscar had but to come up with several hundred gallons of paint. Actually, he had no idea how many gallons of paint it would take to cover the acres of walls inside Bellavista, but that made little difference. He hadn't a penny to spend anyway. He believed the Lord would provide.

One evening, a local evangelical church invited Oscar to tell about the prison ministry and the remarkable changes that were taking place in the jail since the white flag campaign. During his remarks, he mentioned the vision God had given him to repaint the jail. Afterwards, a stranger approached and asked to speak with him.

'I'm a distributor for the Pintuco Paint Company, the largest in Colombia,' the man said. 'I think they might donate some paint for your project, if you present a written request to the management.' The man gave Oscar the names of Pintuco executives to whom he could direct the letter.

Oscar wrote the letter and was granted an interview with the general manager. He arrived at company headquarters ready to explain all about the remarkable change inside

Bellavista, but found he need not bother. The man he had met at the church had already told the Pintuco executives about prisoners laying down their weapons and taking up the Bible. That was, in fact, why the general manager had agreed to see Osorio in the first place.

Oscar got to the point. 'God told me you would give me paint to repaint Bellavista.'

The manager chuckled. 'How much paint do you need?'

'I have no idea,' Oscar said honestly.

'Can you give me an estimate?'

'Sir, I cannot. I only know that God sent me here because he knows you have the paint and that you will give it to me.'

The Pintuco executive looked Oscar in the eye. This man obviously doesn't know much about paint, he thought, but he does seem to know about jails. After a few moments, he said, 'I will have to talk this over with the company board. Why don't you leave me a phone number and I will get back to you.'

The next day the general manager called Oscar and told him his petition had been approved. He could come and collect the paint. When Oscar arrived at the factory, the man pointed him to a Pintuco truck loaded with three tons of paint. 'If that is not enough to do the whole jail, come back,' he said.

Oscar started the prisoners painting. Gangs of inmates sporting T-shirts emblazoned with Scripture texts attacked the spattered walls. The morbid images sketched in congealed blood gradually disappeared under fresh coats of white and pastel. Oscar went back to Pintuco and asked for buckets of black paint. Painters inscribed Bible verses in gigantic block letters over the obscene graffiti. Now when prisoners entered a cell block, John 8.36 greeted them. 'So if the Son makes you free, you will be free indeed.' Inmates who studied in the P3 educational centre could meditate on 2 Corinthians 5.17 while sitting in class: 'Therefore, if anyone is in Christ, he is a new creation; the old has passed away, behold the new has come.'

Bible verses covered the walls of Bellavista. Believers painted huge banners and hung them over the patios, proclaiming

Luke 1.79. 'He gives light to those who sit in darkness and in the shadow of death, to guide our feet into the way of peace.'

All day long, at work, at study, at meals, anywhere they looked, inmates read the Word of God. The power of that Word began to transform the collective psychology of Bellavista.

6

The Bible Behind Bars

Biblical Seminary, April 1991

Early one Monday morning, across town from Bellavista on the tidy campus of the Biblical Seminary, Margarita Henao knocked on Jeannine Brabon's door. Margarita, a student at the Biblical Seminary, explained quietly that her brother, Gustavo, had gone missing several days before. The family had looked everywhere, but found no trace of him. Today Margarita was going to the city morgue to search for her brother. She wondered if, perhaps, Miss Brabon could come along.

Margarita gazed soberly at Jeannine, who stared back as she grasped the implication of the girl's request. Yes, she would go along, Jeannine heard herself say.

Monday being the busiest day of the coroner's week, the two women found the reception area full when they arrived at the city morgue. After stating their business, they were escorted into the cold room. They walked past body after body laid out on the bare concrete, casualties from another long Medellín weekend. Jeannine guessed there were about one hundred laid side by side. All bore marks of violent death.

The women reached the end of the room and started back down the rows of corpses. They finished their grim search and looked silently at one another. Margarita had not found her brother among the dead. Jeannine expected her to be relieved. Instead, the girl said, 'We had better search the morgue in Itagui.'

The Itagui facility on the outskirts of the city was smaller than the downtown morgue. That morning it, too, was crammed with homicide victims. The coroner opened drawers containing the dead for Jeannine and Margarita to examine. He explained that he had received more than 50 bodies the Monday before, at the end of the long Easter weekend. He had had to stack them against the walls. The coroner opened a drawer and Margarita screamed. Her wrenching cry echoed off cold concrete walls.

Jeannine held Margarita in her arms as she sobbed over her brother's corpse. They saw that Gustavo had been tortured. His abductors had burned him with cigarettes and bludgeoned his face before shooting him in the head. He had died five days earlier, the same night he disappeared from home.

The rest of that day passed tediously, consumed by police questioning, forensic reports and the acquisition of the proper documents needed to purchase a casket. The Henao family could not afford to bury Gustavo in a private plot so they arranged for a grave in the pauper cemetery. It was 5 o'clock in the afternoon when the funeral party arrived there.

They were not the only mourners present. As Gustavo's remains were being lowered into the earth, another family wept loudly around an adjacent burial hole. Jeannine noticed the sizeable group was made up mostly of young mothers with small children.

Jeannine lifted her gaze beyond the knot of mourners and saw, stretching away in a neat row, a dozen holes, already dug, waiting. A gloomy thought struck her. Nobody ever called ahead to reserve a burial plot at the pauper cemetery, yet gravediggers knew plenty of clients were on their way here. Jeannine looked around the cemetery and counted at least thirty freshly covered graves. Another long weekend in Medellín.

The simple funeral for Gustavo was nearly finished. Each member of the Henao family tossed the customary handful of earth over the casket as workers filled in the hole. Jeannine heard Gustavo's youngest brother, crying, 'Why Gustavo, why *Gustavo*?' Hoping to comfort the little boy, she touched his shoulder and said, 'Son, this is what took Jesus to the cross.'

Jeannine turned to comfort Margarita. 'This is why Jesus died,' she said to her grieving pupil. 'Don't you see? Because people do these kinds of things to each other, he had to die for us.'

Margarita sobbed and Jeannine put an arm around her. 'He feels your pain,' she whispered, 'Jesus feels your pain.'

Jeannine began to cry, too. As she wept, a question came to her mind. 'What can I do? What *can* I do?' Jeannine wanted to do something to ease the pain for Margarita and her family and all the others ensnared by the death culture. But what could she, an Old Testament Hebrew professor, possibly do?

*   *   *

In February 1991, Carmenza Osorio was working full-time as a homemaker when the Lord directed her to enrol in a Christian Education course at the Biblical Seminary of Colombia. She believed the training would equip her to better support Oscar in his prison ministry. It did.

The same month, the Medellín newspaper *El Colombiano* published a series of feature articles about Oscar's work in the jail under the headline, 'Bellavista Without Homicides'. Nearly a year had passed with no casualties inside the walls, an unprecedented record. The reports on the spiritual awakening that had pacified Colombia's deadliest prison won journalistic acclaim for the author, Mario Carlos Gomez, and attracted the attention of evangelical Christians all over the country.

The stories especially attracted the attention of Jeannine Brabon. When a friend pointed out Carmenza Osorio to her and mentioned that she had enrolled in the seminary, Jeannine made Carmenza's acquaintance and asked to know more about her husband's work. 'Would you like to meet him?' Carmenza suggested.

The next day, Oscar came to the tidy campus of the Biblical Seminary with video clips of TV news reports. Jeannine viewed them in the living room of fellow faculty members Jack and Mary Ann Voelkel. The accounts of Bellavista's *sicarios* and terrorists laying down their weapons and taking up the Bible fascinated the Old Testament professor. 'Would you like to visit the prison tomorrow?' Oscar suggested.

Oscar and Jeannine arranged to meet the following day in the city centre for the drive to Bellavista. On the way, the chaplain asked Jeannine to preach in the worship service that day.

The casual request caught her off guard. 'Who, uh, is my audience?' she asked.

'*Sicarios* and terrorists,' Oscar replied.

Jeannine hesitated. 'What do I know about preaching to men from that kind of background?' she thought to herself. 'We hardly speak the same language. I have absolutely nothing prepared. What if I embarrass myself – and Oscar – on my first visit to Bellavista? Then again, what if this is my *only* visit to Bellavista?'

'Okay, I'll do it,' she said.

Jeannine waited in the jail's anteroom while Oscar talked with the guards and explained the purpose of her visit. She was not the only woman present. Hundreds lined the outer wall of the prison, seeking admittance. Sunday was women's visiting day at Bellavista. It was obvious that many of the females were prostitutes, who bribed the guards to avoid the long wait. Jeannine endured fingerprinting, body searches and curious stares from prison personnel. Few of the women they admitted on Sundays were blond, blue-eyed and conservatively dressed like Jeannine. Finally, they unlocked a series of barred doors admitting her to the prison.

The stench of urine, sweat and rotting food greeted her. She walked close to Oscar through the corridors. On the way the prisoners whistled and flirted. 'Hey, *gringa*, come on in!' She was relieved to reach the chapel where 35 *sicarios* and terrorists waited to begin the worship service. Jeannine recognized Orlando Taborda, who had appeared in the TV news clips. Orlando led the group in hymn singing and prayer. Oscar introduced her to the small congregation. Jeannine swallowed, cleared her throat and clenched her fists.

'I wonder if you know what the word "mercy" means,' she

said, trying her best to conceal the tremor in her voice. 'To illustrate, I would like to tell you a story about King David of Israel. The Bible describes him as "a man after God's own heart". He was the finest ruler his country would ever know. Nevertheless, he had enemies.'

Jeannine narrated the story of David's conflict with the jealous Saul, who tried several times to kill the young man because he sensed David would some day be king in his place. David's best friend, oddly enough, was Jonathan, Saul's eldest son and the next in line to the throne.

Jeannine recounted the tragic events at Mount Gilboa, when the Philistines massacred Saul, Jonathan and nearly all their male relatives. Saul's downfall and Jonathan's death opened the way for David to become king. When he was firmly enthroned, he brought Mephibosheth, Jonathan's son, to court.

'Mephibosheth's name in Hebrew means "man of shame".' Jeannine explained. 'He lived in Lodebar, which literally translated means "nowhere". He was crippled and impoverished. What's more, he was the grandson of David's mortal enemy. The custom of the day called for kings to annihilate all rivals. Mephibosheth, in other words, was as good as dead.'

Jeannine noticed that the Bellavista inmates were listening intently to her story. They nodded their heads knowingly when Jeannine mentioned annihilation of enemies. It gave her goose bumps.

'But David had experienced the love of God,' Jeannine said. 'The Hebrews have a special word for it: *hesed*. We translate it as "loving-kindness". It is a steadfast love that never ceases, no matter how badly we behave or how little we deserve it.

'Instead of killing Mephibosheth, David showed *hesed* to the unfortunate man. He brought him from Lodebar to live in Jerusalem. Its name means "City of peace". Every day Mephibosheth ate at David's own table, with his own family.

'When you see how David showed loving-kindness to Mephibosheth, you see a picture of God's mercy. God loves every one of us in exactly the same way, no matter how badly we behave or how little we deserve it.'

Jeannine concluded her remarks and sat down. Oscar stood up and spoke briefly to the group. He explained that anyone who wished to receive God's mercy could stand to his feet. Twenty-three *sicarios* and terrorists stood up, tears streaming down their faces. Oscar, Orlando and other believers prayed the prayer of faith with the men.

When they finished, Oscar told Jeannine he would like her to visit a cell block called La Guayana. He led her up to the top floor of the prison and through a heavy iron door. Jeannine held her breath because of the stench. 'It's because there are no toilets here,' Oscar explained frankly.

Oscar and Jeannine began to sing hymns and read Scripture texts to La Guayana inmates. Some of them sang along, some shed tears, all of them pressed their faces against the bars of the cramped cells to hear better. After a while, the duty officer came down the corridor unlocking cell doors so the prisoners of La Guayana could take their one hour of daily exercise. The 50 assassins crowded around Jeannine and Oscar. Oddly, she sensed the presence of angels.

As they were leaving Bellavista, Jeannine plied Oscar with questions about his work in the jail. She discovered that Prison Fellowship in Medellín had dwindled. Oscar was one of the few left of its volunteer staff. Manuel Casteñeda had ceased visiting the prison to give more time to his halfway house. The Covenant Evangelical Mission had withdrawn their missionaries, Gwyn Lewis and Javier and Victor Celis, two years before. After six years with the Bellavista ministry, Francisco Archila resigned as director. Happily, Luz Elena Torres still directed the P3 educational centre.

Despite the decline in Prison Fellowship volunteers, a revival was flourishing among the inmates. Oscar estimated that over 300 prisoners were participating in daily Bible study sessions. Of those, he identified dozens with potential to become pastors and evangelists. Some were already shepherding the church behind bars. Few were educated men. Most had the equivalent of a primary school education, Oscar reckoned. But he knew they would apply themselves if given the chance for proper theological training.

He fixed a steady gaze on Jeannine.'Will you help me train leaders?' he asked.

'How could I?' Jeannine thought to herself.'What would we use for curriculum? I have no idea what they need to know to be effective in prison ministry. The inmates seem to have a lot of enthusiasm right now, but it's possible that interest will die, once they realize how demanding serious theological training is.'

Then Jeannine remembered. She had heard the voice of God calling her back to Colombia, she had no doubt about that. He must have his reasons. Could Bellavista be one of them?

'Okay, I'll do it,' she said.

*   *   *

Jeannine started spending two days a week inside Bellavista. In Cell Block Eight, Orlando Taborda took advantage of her visits to sharpen his understanding of the Bible. As a 24-hour prison pastor, Taborda needed to keep himself sharp spiritually.

I prayed to God often that he would send us persons to build up leaders. I was seeing many of the believers back-slide and it worried me. God sent us an angel – that's what I call her – Jeannine. She came from heaven.

The day they introduced me to her, Jeannine taught me a message on death. I will never forget the passage: 1 Corinthians 15. She told me about her father's death. She said that death was the Christian's greatest prize. The Bible says,'O death, where is thy sting?' The sting of death is sin. If someone passes away without sin, he or she steps out into the best moment of life, right into the presence of God. That was a great message for my life.

Many Christian groups had heard of the glory of God in the prison. Every type of evangelical – at least they had the evangelical label – began to visit us. But they did us more harm than good. The majority of them arrived for a little while and soon disappeared. The only ones who remained were Brother Oscar and Sister Jeannine.

Jeannine Brabon sat at a table surrounded by solemn men and women representing the Association of Medellín Evangelical Ministers and other Christian groups which were in one way or another involved in prison ministry. Several months had passed since her first visit to Bellavista and she was explaining to them her idea of establishing an extension of the Biblical Seminary inside the jail.

Jeannine understood that her dream of a jailhouse Bible college faced serious difficulties. When she first presented the plan to her colleagues at the Biblical Seminary of Colombia, their professional response was . . . laughter. Realizing she was serious, Vice-Rector Theo Donner cautiously consented to help her develop a plan. However, he suggested, any project of this nature should have the blessing of the entire Medellín evangelical community. That was why she now sat at a table surrounded by solemn men and women.

Jeannine outlined her idea. Students from the Biblical Seminary would teach theology classes in Bellavista and receive academic credit in return. She pointed out that seminary students would confront the death culture in communities where they worked after graduation, so why not help them now to develop the necessary skills to do so? She mentioned that several seminary students were learning about the death culture through volunteer work with the football clubs that Mark Wittig operated. Many of the teenage players they had brought to Christ would likely be *sicarios* themselves by now, had they not joined one of Mark's clubs.

The solemn men and women listened with interest to what Jeannine was saying. But she wondered if her pitch really convinced them. She knew that several of the group had been working in prison ministries much longer than she herself.

'Do you really think you are going to find theology students willing to teach the Bible to fellows who have killed 100 people?' one of them asked.

It was a fair question. Jeannine took a deep breath and said, 'It's a difficult situation, no doubt about it. When I first started visiting the prison, I felt the tension myself. I know some of the families of their victims.' The image of Gustavo Henao, lying mutilated in the morgue, flashed through Jeannine's mind.

'A few weeks ago, Jack and Mary Ann Voelkel conducted an inner healing seminar inside the jail,' she continued. 'We learned a lot about the prisoners' past, the poverty, the abuse. To see where they've come from, to feel their pain, and then to see the power of God at work . . . well, the Lord just gives you a love for them.'

It was an honest answer. The solemn men and women sitting at the table understood just how honest. They asked Jeannine more questions about her Bible seminary proposal, questions about curriculum, academic standards, follow-up with graduates – all the right sorts of questions. The longer they talked, it seemed to Jeannine, the less solemn they became.

Evidently they were satisfied with Jeannine's answers. Before the meeting adjourned, she found herself appointed to an interdenominational committee and entrusted with establishing the Bellavista Bible Institute.

Bellavista National Jail, January 1994

José Giraldo, 27 years old, is two years into a 20-year sentence for armed robbery, kidnap and extortion. Bright, energetic and articulate, José is not the sort of young man one expects to meet in prison. He leans against a barred window inside Bellavista and begins to tell his story.

When I was five years old, my life took a turn for the worse. Father suffered a financial failure. We came to Medellín to try our luck, but our situation grew desperate. We constructed a shack of sticks and plastic sheets on the mountainside above the city. We survived in this way for three long years, until we could construct a real house.

I excelled academically in school, but spent most of my time fighting. To help finance my education, I took temporary jobs washing cars, selling cigarettes and shining shoes. I was extremely rebellious. I withdrew from secondary school lacking only one year to finish. My sister, Elizabeth, was converted to Christ and began to pray earnestly for my regeneration. Every chance she got, she talked to me about the grace of God. I liked hearing the gospel but my ambitions got me sidetracked.

I enlisted in the army, hoping that military life would give form to my disorganized life. But what I experienced in the armed forces only disillusioned me further. While in the barracks I learned of my mother's death. Shattered and unstable, I nursed the idea of suicide. Fortunately, a sergeant counselled me and warded off a disaster.

Our home split up after my mother's death. I returned to civilian life and started working as a bodyguard in an upmarket neighbourhood, the 'El Poblado' district. I worked for a man who owns several businesses in Medellín, looking after his wife and kids. That's really when I started my criminal career because I began having lots of money, guns, cars and women. I became a promiscuous man, a drinking man.

In 1987, I got into trouble with the Mafia. One of the gangs of the Medellín cartel stole two thousand kilos of cocaine base from another gang. I was passing by in the car at the exact moment they were unloading the drugs from a truck. I got a look at it and they got a look at me. You can imagine what happened. One gang was threatening me not to tell that they were the ones who stole the shipment and another gang was going to kill me for not telling them who stole it. I was between a rock and a hard place. I had to get out of there.

I left my job and joined a band of organized criminals. We committed robberies and bank hold-ups. In 1990 we planned a jewellery shop robbery that turned into a kidnapping. My partners called me and said, 'José, we abducted the son of the jewellery shop owner.' I said, 'Why in the world did you do that?' 'Look, take it easy,' they said. 'We are going to make more money with him. We just need you to guard him for two hours.' They took me to a certain place in Medellín and left me with the boy.

The boy and I started talking and pretty soon we were friends. I was thinking, if it falls to me to kill this boy – who was 15 and in school – I don't know what I'll do. Thankfully, two hours later my partners arrived and took him away to a farm outside Medellín.

A few days later, my companions called to say it was time to collect the ransom. The most dangerous part of a kidnapping is receiving the money. I wanted to show that I was fearless and thus move up in the ranks of the gang, so I went to collect it. That's when the security forces captured me – with 100 million pesos of ransom money. Generally, they kill the fellow they catch with the ransom, but they didn't kill me. I managed to drop a paper on the sidewalk with my home phone number on it, so that somebody would call my family and tell them I had been arrested. Evidently, somebody did.

Not all of the security forces are bad, but some are not too, ah, proper. They will do things like put a plastic bag over your head until you nearly suffocate, or clamp a pair of pliers onto your genitals. They tortured me. They made me play Russian roulette. It's a kind of psychological torture.

They hauled me from place to place, demanding information about the people I worked with. It's a big trap you're in. If you give them information, the people you work with will kill your family. Or they may send somebody to jail to kill you. I told the police nothing, so they were getting ready to 'disappear' me. They know that if your relatives have no knowledge of your arrest, they can kill you any time they want.

That was the most terrifying part. At one point, the police were carrying me across town in the boot of a car. I remembered something my sister Elizabeth told me. If ever I were in trouble, I should say, 'Blood of Jesus, cover me.' I was having an emotional crisis at that moment, so I said, 'Blood of Jesus, cover me, protect me. Lord, give me another chance. I'll change.'

The police didn't disappear me. I learned later that my sister Elizabeth was asking about me in all the offices of the security forces. She even looked for me in the morgue. My family was mourning my death, but Elizabeth was certain I was still alive. She went to one police station and talked to the duty officer. She kept insisting until the man decided to go back into the most secluded calaboose to ask if there was a person there by the name of José Giraldo. I was there and answered him. The duty officer went out and told my sister that I was being detained, but he did not understand why my name was not listed in the arrest logbook. I knew why. They were going to get the information they wanted and then kill me. Thanks to my sister's persistence, they didn't. God did a marvellous work there. It caused me to believe the gospel is true.

When I arrived at Bellavista prison, my life was in danger once again. I was in trouble with the gang, who thought I had given information to the police. I was scared to death.

They assigned me to Patio Eight, cell number 20. A group of brothers got together to sing that night, and I was able to hear the hymns. I liked them very much. The next day, they asked me if I wanted to accept Christ. I said, 'No, I'm going to take it slow on that decision.' They talked to me about the Bible. I asked to borrow one. I started reading it and the Lord touched me powerfully. He transformed my life.

I started meeting with Christians in the cell block. Orlando Taborda was there, a grand servant of God. The fact that he had been a criminal and had changed helped me a great deal. I realized I could be a different person through Jesus. I began every day poring over the Scriptures. I had a desire to read more and know more.

Orlando asked me to help him share the Word with my old friends who were now in jail. One of them was the boss of a powerful Medellín gang. He laughed at me and said, 'You're not capable of truly giving yourself to Jesus.' He asked me to help him smuggle weapons into the jail. But I told him, 'I'm not doing that any more, friend. I'm seeking Jesus.' Over time, he finally learned to respect me.

I shared the Word with several people in the cell block and many of them accepted Jesus. I would preach a lot on the verse Matthew 11.28. Men who are incarcerated are beaten down by life. We are dealing with lots of problems. That keeps us constantly tense, anxious, depressed. Coming to Jesus is a relief. You realize that it's not mere words. It's reality.

Medellín, February 1992

Renzo Espinoza, a fourth-year student at the Biblical Seminary of Colombia, watched two armed teenagers work their way down the aisle of the Medellín city bus. Renzo had felt nervous all during the bus ride across town. Jeannine Brabon had recruited him to teach a New Testament course in the Bellavista Bible Institute. He was on his way to the prison for his first class. That was why he felt nervous. The thought of spending several hours a week inside Colombia's deadliest prison was enough to make anyone nervous. The thought of falling victim to armed robbery on the way to the jail had not occurred to Renzo. But it was happening now as if he were in the middle of a bad dream.

No one on the bus had noticed the two teenagers until they whipped out pistols and announced the hold-up. While one pointed his weapon at passengers' heads, the other held a bag into which each one emptied money and valuables. They moved from seat to seat. The bag got heavier, the mood got tenser. Renzo dreaded his turn. He had come from his native Ecuador to study at the Biblical Seminary and barely had enough money to cover school bills and living expenses. He could not afford to empty his pockets.

Just as the bandits reached Renzo's seat, they stopped abruptly and peered out of the window. The frightened expressions on their faces indicated that something was amiss, although Renzo could not see what it was. The two stuck their guns into their trousers, turned and fled. Renzo sighed with relief and bowed his head to thank God for the last-minute deliverance.

The Bellavista Bible Institute had opened for business. Twenty-one students enrolled in the first semester of studies.

In addition to Renzo, Jeannine Brabon recruited Lacides Hernandez, Fabian Cortez, Simy Rivera and other students and faculty from the Biblical Seminary to teach theology classes. Renzo's narrow escape from the bus bandits on the first day's commute turned out to be the greatest danger any of them faced during the semester. The teachers found they were safer among the *sicarios* and terrorists inside Bellavista than on the streets of Medellín. Since the white flag campaign two years earlier, not a single casualty had been reported inside the prison. It was an unprecedented record for Colombia's deadliest jail.

Calarca, September 1991

Three months after Jeannine Brabon taught him about the Christian hope of eternal life, Orlando Taborda was transferred out of Bellavista to another prison.

They sent me to Calarca, a very tough jail, but the Lord Jesus was already at work. They assigned me to the worst cell block. The fellows had a big grudge against those of us who came from Bellavista. For me, it was like Daniel in the lion's den. God closed up the mouths of all those lions. They surrounded me, but nobody dared take me down.

There were 50 fellows in the cell block. The first day, I started sharing about the Lord with each one individually. I said, 'Day after tomorrow, I'm going to preach the Bible to anybody who wants to listen.' A small group formed. I prayed to God that they would let me preach in other cell blocks. They didn't. I kept praying.

After one year in Calarca, they let me go into all the cell blocks to preach. Brother Oscar and Jeannine came to visit me. God raised up a church there of 70 believers. I started training leaders, teaching them to tithe and to organize the church. A fellow called El Caleño said he was going to kill me, that I was a *sapo*. I told him, 'The day God permits you to do that, it's because he has a better gift for me.' God never permitted it.

I received a notice that, due to changes in the constitution of Colombia, I was entitled to a reduction of sentence. They took me to a prison in Andes, a community near Medellín. The day I arrived there, I talked to the governor and asked his permission to preach. He asked me two questions, one about Psalm 23 and the other about Psalm 91. He said, 'I'm going to give you two days a week.' So I started to share with the fellows and a little church was raised up there.

Six months later, I was granted my freedom. I served a total of 50 months, three days, one hour and a half. I left prison without a penny. But I came out with something I never could have bought with money – eternal life. I began working as a volunteer in Bellavista Jail, helping Brother Oscar in the ministry.

I had no place to live. I couldn't stay at my mother's place because people were looking for me to kill me. Several times they telephoned to tell me they were going to kill me. In one call, the sister of the last fellow I killed said that if I stopped preaching, she wouldn't have me assassinated. 'Don't talk about God,' she said. 'You are not a person to talk about God.' I said, 'Look, I used to risk my life to commit crimes. If they kill me now on account of the gospel, well, it's a blessing.'

I don't care if I die. I ask God to make it soon. I have said, 'Lord, just let me talk about Jesus Christ to the fellow who is going to take my life, so that he will repent and find salvation.' After that, he can kill me, I don't care. It would be my best gift.

7

Prison Missionaries

In the spring of 1992, some weeks after the inauguration of the Bellavista Bible Institute, Fabian Cortez had some disturbing news for Jeannine Brabon. Oscar Osorio was no longer working in the prison. No one knew why, but the chaplain had abruptly disappeared from the jail.

Jeannine wasted no time. She sought out Carmenza Osorio and asked if anything was amiss with her husband. Carmenza told her that he had taken a permanent job in the building trade in order to support the family and pay her tuition at the Biblical Seminary. But what about the salary he received from the Covenant Evangelical Mission? Jeannine asked. Didn't that money provide their living expenses? Yes, it had, Carmenza said, but Oscar was no longer receiving the salary. The Covenant Evangelical Church had dismissed him as a minister. That was why he took the construction job.

Jeannine phrased her next question delicately. What if, say, another salary could be raised? she asked. Would Oscar return to his prison ministry? Of course he would return, Carmenza said. Jeannine was relieved that Oscar's absence from Bellavista was merely an economic issue and had nothing to do with exhaustion or discouragement.

She asked Carmenza to talk with Oscar and calculate their family budget. Jeannine arranged to meet the couple for lunch to discuss the amount of money they needed each month to pay their bills. The three of them established a salary figure and entered into a covenant. Oscar would resume his daily ministry inside Bellavista, Carmenza would continue her studies in the Biblical Seminary and Jeannine would join them in trusting the Lord to provide the money they needed to pay their bills.

As it turned out, events over the next few months led to the revival of Medellín's moribund Prison Fellowship, which had practically ceased operations following the resignation of Francisco Archila. A few weeks after her lunch with the Osorios, Jeannine accepted an invitation from Guillermo Novoa, director of Prison Fellowship of Colombia, to attend a meeting of the national board of directors in Bogotá. Novoa and his colleagues heard about the remarkable progress in Bellavista and decided to charter a new chapter of the organization. Although Prison Fellowship did not provide financial support for the Bellavista staff, their endorsement made it possible for Jeannine to solicit donations from churches and individuals. Jeannine accepted the assignment of organizing the new chapter, known as Prison Fellowship of Antioquia.

Prison Fellowship of Antioquia was legally registered with the Colombian government in June 1993. Renzo Espinoza, Lacides Hernandez and Fabian Cortez joined Jeannine and Oscar on the board of directors. Donations to the new chapter provided money to operate the Bellavista Bible Institute and provide a monthly salary for Oscar Osorio. He, Carmenza and Jeannine had trusted the Lord and, once again, the Lord had provided.

* * *

José Giraldo, bright, energetic and articulate, was one of the first inmates to enrol in the Bellavista Bible Institute. José had already begun pastoring the church behind bars when the new school opened.

I had been living in the Word of God eight months when Orlando Taborda was transferred to another jail. He told me I would be leading a group of 30 fellows. I was scared to death. How could I be in charge? I didn't know how to preach. But all of the brothers in the cell block backed me, even the *cacique*.

I began rising at 4 a.m. to spend time in fasting and prayer. I would pray until late hours of the night, asking for guidance. I lost a great deal of weight. During this time, a blond missionary with a different accent came to the jail. She was Jeannine Brabon. I asked her for advice about helping the brothers. She responded wholeheartedly.

In company with other brothers, I studied in the Bellavista Bible Institute to teach the Word with greater effectiveness. It would take me a great deal of time to describe what the Bible Institute has meant to my life. I came to know men like Fabian Cortez, the first academic dean and a great friend. Renzo Espinoza and Lacides Hernandez were also great friends and counsellors. Oscar Osorio is a man of God who has always been an inspiration to me. God bless them for their time and effort.

Luz Elena Torres, the director of the P3 educational centre opened another opportunity for me. She placed me in charge of a non-formal education class, a group of 80 or 90 men. We held seminars on topics like human relations, family life, sexuality and drug abuse. There was a course on religion in which I took the opportunity to share the Good News. Through the P3 programme, several hundred persons have come to know Jesus. Many have gone through the Bible Institute. Our desire is that not just 20 or 30 or 70, but that all the thousands of inmates in Bellavista might know Jesus.

I got to know Luz Dary Ocampo before going to jail. We have a beautiful boy, José Daniel, who was born during my imprisonment. When I became a Christian, Luz Dary really reacted against the Word. She was harsh with me. I said, 'Luz Dary, even if you don't give your life to the Lord, we can stay together. I'm a son of God now and that would please my Father.' I waited patiently and the Lord worked in her life.

We decided to get married. In 1994, Pastor Oscar Osorio performed our wedding in the Bellavista prison chapel. My wife has been a great blessing to my life. She married a man condemned to 20 years, agreeing to wait for him all that time. Meanwhile she began attending a Christian congregation where she served as an usher and Sunday school teacher. She could only come to visit me every fortnight because the other Sundays she was at church.

For a long time, I asked myself: If I am freed, what career am I going to pursue? I have lots of friends who are engineers, doctors and architects. But God taught me something in the days after I received my 20-year sentence. I said to Jesus, 'I don't want to be an architect nor the best doctor there is. I want to be your servant, Lord, and serve you here in Bellavista.'

*   *   *

In 1990, Pablo Escobar declared all-out war on law enforcement. The word went out to *sicarios* in Medellín slums: The *Patron* will pay $4,000 dollars for every dead cop, $8,000 for a member of the élite narcotics squad. Ambitious *pistoleros* began killing constables, detectives, traffic patrolmen – anyone in a uniform.

Few of the gunmen were aware that they were actually engaged in a private vendetta. In the early hours of a March morning, police raided an apartment in the fashionable El Poblado district occupied by Mrs Victoria Eugenia Escobar and her two children. The officers questioned the woman about the whereabouts of her husband, Colombia's most wanted criminal.

The police action infuriated Pablo Escobar, who was also Colombia's richest criminal. According to his peculiar code of ethics, the authorities had no right to involve his family in the drug war. Escobar's criminal organization had left hundreds of women widowed and children orphaned, but in his mind, his own household was untouchable. The police would pay for this outrage. Over the next four months, 250 Medellín police officers paid with their lives.

The vendetta would change forever the life of Officer Fernando Arroyave. Although he knew nothing of the raid on the Escobar apartment in El Poblado and had little interest in war of any kind, the amiable 26-year-old policeman with a boyish grin and a reputation for decency was soon caught in the middle of the violence.

I worked six years on the police force, for five of those years, honourably. In 1990, I was the victim of two murder attempts. I took two bullets in one assault, one on the left side near the heart and another in my leg.

From that moment on I was angry. Some of my colleagues invited me to go with them to take revenge. First they sent me out to steal a public taxi. I went with another officer. We dressed in civilian clothes and wore sunglasses to hide our identities. Later, I watched my companions kill people. Some young fellows were standing on a street corner drinking alcohol and listening to music. We drove up in the taxi, threw them on the ground and proceeded to shoot them.

I did not take part at first because I was shy and afraid. I'm a country boy, you see. Honest, hard-working, poor, but from a good family. My mate said to me, 'Since you're scared, come over here.' He put his hand over mine on the gun and pulled the trigger for me. I saw the fellow die on the street. He pumped more bullets into him, but the boy was already dead.

That's how I was initiated into the criminal life. Within eight months, I turned into one of the most respected killers in Medellín. Actually, people did not respect me, they dreaded me. I had become an evil man, ready at any minute to take another human being's life for revenge, for money, and ultimately for sheer pleasure.

I killed around sixty people. My commanding officers started investigating me. I was afraid to go to work because I knew they were going to order my arrest. So I took 45 vacation days that were coming to me and never went back. The security forces started a manhunt. The national police, the secret police, even a contingent of the Fourth Army Brigade all had their orders to take me down wherever they found me.

The people in my neighbourhood looked at me as if I was some kind of stranger, not the fellow they used to know: modest, cheerful, always doing people favours. Those looks provoked a horrible panic inside me. My friends did not hang out with me any more. They knew that if they were around when my enemies caught up with me, they would get killed, too. The popular militias (the vigilante groups that shoot thieves in my neighbourhood) gave my family 24 hours to get out of the house we had lived in for 25 years. It was all my fault.

My life was chaos. I was possessed by a malignant spirit. I must have delighted the devil a great deal. Near the end, something terrible happened to me. I had to kill in order to relax. If a day passed in which I had not murdered somebody, I could not fall asleep that night.

Bogotá, September 1992

Jeannine Brabon sat in front of a burnished, mahogany desk in the Bogotá office of Colombia's top lawman, Gustavo De Greiff, Prosecutor General of the Nation. Across from her sat De Greiff, puffing incessantly on a pipe and talking on the telephone.

Colombia had created the post of Prosecutor General in 1990. The new constitution endued the office with broad powers. When the Council of State appointed De Greiff as the first Prosecutor General, the ministers granted him authority to reshape the country's three existing security agencies into an effective national police force. De Greiff also had power to overhaul Colombia's antiquated judicial system. The measures were necessary if De Greiff were to accomplish the mandate which parliament, the judiciary, President César Gaviria and the Colombian people had given him: stamp out terrorism, win the drug war and hunt down Pablo Escobar.

De Greiff had made some headway, at least in his fight against the Medellín cartel. His field agents had pieced together intelligence on Escobar and his *sicario* network. An élite squad of investigators was tightening the noose around the drug lord and his hideouts in Antioquia. The Prosecutor General had amassed evidence of his numerous crimes, so that when and if Escobar were captured, the justice system could convict him.

Gustavo De Greiff had attracted considerable attention for his accomplishments. The press admired him for his candid honesty as much as for his relentless pursuit of criminals. The prestigious Bogotá news magazine *Semana* named him Man of the Year for 1992 and commended him for 'restoring credibility to the Colombian justice system'. Most of the attention De Greiff attracted, however, was of a more sinister nature. Colombia's criminals considered him their most dangerous adversary. Because of the constant threat of assassination, the government assigned De Greiff two fleets of armoured limousines. Each evening as he left his office, both fleets sped out of the underground parking lot by different exits and in opposite directions, surrounded by police escorts, sirens blaring. One caravan carried the Prosecutor General, always by a different route, to his home. The other served as a decoy. Some evenings, both served as decoys and De Greiff slipped out unobtrusively and made his own way home.

As Jeannine Brabon sat across the mahogany desk from De Greiff waiting for him to finish the phone call, she realized how little he looked like a powerful lawman. He much more resembled what he had been before becoming Prosecutor General: Rector of the University of Rosario. The slight, bespectacled man puffing on his pipe and squinting at the person on the other end of the telephone was the very image of the cultivated scholar. A crucifix hanging above his desk completed the picture of Gustavo De Greiff, a decent, God-fearing citizen doing his patriotic duty. The cross also represented De Greiff's primary motive for accepting the post of Prosecutor General. Once a reporter asked him how he was able to cope with the staggering pressures of the job. 'The only thing that gives me strength to do this work is the conviction that I am contributing to the work of God on earth,' he replied.

Gustavo De Greiff recruited the best available talent to staff his new law enforcement office. A key member of his team was Martha Castro, a veteran judicial adviser in the Ministry of Justice. Dr Castro joined the Prosecutor General's office in July 1992, a few months after she was baptized at the Unicentro Fellowship Church.

Martha had accepted Jesus Christ a year earlier through

the influence of Patricia Martinez, her assistant at the Ministry of Justice. In 1990, Patricia married Dr David Brabon, a Bogotá plastic surgeon. The couple invited Martha Castro to their wedding. It was the first time she had ever attended a Protestant church, but the wedding ceremony greatly impressed Dr Castro. She told David and Patricia that when, soon after returning from their honeymoon, the couple invited her to dinner, the three spent most of the evening discussing the gospel. Afterwards, Martha Castro prayed the prayer of faith.

A few months later, David and Patricia Brabon introduced her to David's younger sister, Jeannine, who told Martha about the remarkable revival inside Bellavista prison. The veteran judicial adviser was so impressed by the accounts of *sicarios* and terrorists laying down their weapons to take up the Bible that she made an appointment for Jeannine to speak with her boss, Gustavo De Greiff. Dr Castro believed it might encourage him to know what God was doing in one of Colombia's deadliest prisons. That was why Jeannine Brabon was sitting across the burnished mahogany desk from Colombia's most powerful lawman.

De Greiff hung up the telephone and apologized to his guest for the delay. 'Now, tell me about what you do,' he said.

Jeannine started by explaining her decision to return from Spain to Medellín. 'I wanted to do something, whatever I could, to help people deal with the death culture,' she said. 'I didn't want to just teach, but to touch people's lives somehow. That's how God led me into Bellavista prison.'

De Greiff removed the pipe from his lips and sat up in his chair. 'That's the most dangerous prison in the country,' he said.

'It was. Would you like to know what God is doing there?'

'Yes, I would.'

Jeannine told about Oscar Osorio and his preaching in the prison. She described the peculiar but effective white flag campaign that quelled a riot and sparked a revival. 'The reason Bellavista is peaceful,' she said, 'is because inmates – even some of the *caciques* – have experienced the power of God in their lives. The first thing many of the men want to do after meeting Christ is to straighten out their family life. We have celebrated several weddings in the prison chapel. Many broken homes have been restored, which is exciting for us. We network with churches in the area where these families live and they invite them to their worship services.'

Jeannine laid a piece of paper on his desk. 'This is a letter to you from a prisoner in Bellavista,' she said. 'I think you might want to read it.'

De Greiff picked it up and read.

Dr Gustavo De Greiff
Prosecutor General of the Nation

Doctor,
With all the respect that you and your office deserve, I salute you in the name of our Lord and Saviour Jesus Christ. Prompted by the disturbing situation which our country faces and because of the great difficulty of the task you perform, I dared write to you to encourage you to be strengthened in Christ, to fight for justice and truth.

My name is Orlando Taborda. I was born into a home disobedient to God. I made a profession of evil, eventually becoming a *sicario*. I only lived to hate the authorities, because I knew many, from politicians to policemen, who were corrupt. My life was a void. I found only pleasure, never happiness. I was imprisoned for homicide and illegal possession of arms. I thought of suicide as a solution. But a man talked to me and presented Christ as the solution. Thirty-six months ago, condemned to prison and penniless, I found freedom.

Respected Doctor, out of regard for your prestigious and dangerous position, I want to say to you that there is no more honourable man than the one who governs in the fear of God. A group of brothers in this penitentiary want to say that not all of us are your enemies. We are praying that God will bless you and protect you from every evil. We are your friends and desire to be your brothers in Christ.

Sincerely,
Orlando Taborda
Rural Penitentiary
Calarca, Colombia

The Prosecutor General finished reading and sat quietly. He pondered how these men – criminals who should consider Gustavo De Greiff their most dangerous adversary – could ask God to protect his life and bless his work. It was nothing short of a marvel.

'I found out some time ago that there had been a change in that prison,' he remarked, 'but I didn't know how the change happened. Now I do.'

'Dr De Greiff, may I pray with you right now?' Jeannine asked.

'Thank you, I would like that,' he said.

Jeannine Brabon got up and walked around behind the Prosecutor General's chair. She laid her hands gently on his shoulders and prayed. When she finished, she returned to her seat across the desk from Gustavo De Greiff. He said, a bit hoarsely, 'When do you come back to Bogotá again?'

'I come about once a month,' she replied.

'When you do, stop by, will you?'

'Surely.'

Then something happened which was quite out of character for Colombia's most powerful lawman. The dangerous adversary of terrorists and *sicarios*, hunter of Pablo Escobar, Man of the Year who had restored credibility to the Colombian justice system, brushed tears from his eyes.

Medellín, August 1991

Fernando Arroyave, the young policeman who, in the space of eight months, had turned into a reckless *sicario*, reached the very bottom of his private hell.

I kept murdering and stealing, leading a horrible life. I only thought about killing anyone who could testify against me. If I saw one of them on the street, I chased him down and took his life. I murdered a man the night I was arrested. It was a night like any other. I was in a public house in the city at 4 a.m. I was drunk. In those last days I got myself drunk constantly in order not to feel them closing in on me.

They caught me and I went to Bellavista prison. Every

criminal in Medellín was in that jail. I couldn't live with those fellows because I had formerly belonged to the police force. So they assigned me to a special cell block, Number Eleven. One afternoon, Jeannine Brabon came there.

She gave me a Bible. She invited me to a course on inner healing that was being held in the chapel. She came constantly to visit me in the cell block to talk to me about Christ. I didn't know what it was all about. Like Saul, I was a practised persecutor of people who preached the gospel. I used to curse the evangelicals. However, I felt something strange when Jeannine started talking to me about Christ, saying she wanted me to give my life to him. I endured our chats because it was pleasant having her around. Jeannine inspires confidence, tranquillity. I talked to her because of what she radiated.

She kept visiting me once a week, talking to me about the Word, until I accepted Christ. When I gave myself to the Lord, he began working on me. I was freed. I'm serving a 29-year sentence, but the happiest days of my life have been the ones since I have known Jesus. The peace I always craved, I have now. He's the only one who could do that for me.

Bogotá, October 1992

Jeannine Brabon sat in the Bogotá office of Colonel Gustavo Socha Salamanca, Director General of Prisons. She had come to ask the colonel a favour. There was a problem at the Bellavista Bible Institute. Of the 25 students who enrolled the first year, exactly three completed their courses. It was not because the rest lost interest, as Jeannine had feared they might. They all had left Bellavista for other jails.

'Because Bellavista is a holding facility where prisoners remain only until assigned permanently to other penitentiaries, our students were transferred before completing their studies,' Jeannine explained to the colonel. 'We wonder if something can be done to keep them in Bellavista longer.'

The Director General listened with interest. He had cancelled the first two interviews Jeannine scheduled with him, first, because of his busy schedule and second, because he received too many requests for interviews from people asking favours. He agreed to see Miss Brabon today for one reason. Gustavo De Greiff, Colombia's most powerful lawman, had alerted the colonel that the woman had some important things to tell him. After De Greiff's call, Colonel Socha telegrammed Jeannine 'reiterating my desire to cooperate with the programmes that are developing'. That was why she was sitting in his Bogotá office.

Like De Greiff, Colonel Socha knew about the remarkable drop in the homicide rate inside Bellavista. The jail had not recorded a single murder in nearly three years, an unprecedented record among Colombian prisons. The Director General was keenly interested in how the deadliest prison under his jurisdiction had suddenly become the safest. Today he was learning how.

Jeannine described Oscar's work in the jail, mentioning that over 300 inmates were meeting each day in Bible study groups. Scores of prisoners spent regular time in fasting and prayer. Several of them were preaching daily to their fellow inmates in the cell blocks. Jeannine concluded by stating her personal conviction that God had taken Bellavista in his hand. That was why the killing had stopped.

Jeannine then described the aims of the Bellavista Bible Institute and her dream of giving Christian inmates a solid theological education. Jailhouse pastors need solid training, she said, to deal with the enormous pressures they face. Wouldn't the colonel agree?

The colonel did agree. Like few other men, he grasped the significance of the spiritual awakening inside Bellavista. He also appreciated its potential for improving conditions in other jails. As Jeannine talked, a plan took shape in the Director General's mind.

'Look, I'm the man that signs the papers authorizing prisoner transfers,' he told the two. 'Give me a list of the inmates you are training, and when you have them ready to go, let me know. Tell me what prison you want me to send them to, if you have a preference. Otherwise we'll send them to the ones that most need the, ah, changes you have described. I think we might be able to work together on this.'

On her next visit to Bellavista, Jeannine went to Cell Block Eleven to see Fernando Arroyave and encourage him to enrol in the Bible Institute's second-year class of 21 students. Fernando had begun preaching the gospel to the police and military officers incarcerated in his cell block.

'Fernando, I don't want you to look at the 29 years ahead of you in prison,' she said. 'Instead, take these next two years to learn all you can about the Bible. Allow God to mould your character. After that, we are going to send you as an apostle to another penitentiary.'

Tears welled up in Fernando's eyes. 'You mean, God could use *me*?'

Jeannine nodded.

'I suppose if God could take a Saul, transform the violence in his soul and make him into an apostle, he could do the same for me,' he said. 'If he calls, I am willing to go.'

Before the year was out, God would call Fernando. The ex-policeman with the boyish grin and sixty homicides in his past would join Adán Colorado, Orlando Taborda and José Giraldo in a growing company of Bellavista missionaries.

Bellavista, May 1997

If Gilberto Paez, 26, were cast in a cops-and-robbers movie, he would take the part of the hero. Blond, trim and virile, he resembles a typical idol of the cinema.

One morning in December 1993, he sat in the patio of his cell block in Bellavista Jail peeling potatoes and tried to muster the courage to cut his own throat with the knife.

'Gilberto Paez' was actually an alias the young man adopted while working for the Medellín drug cartel. The youngest of 13 children, he grew up in the borough of Aranjuez, a working-class neighbourhood that provided the cartel with a steady stream of teenage recruits. At 16, Gilberto joined a band of *sicarios* assigned to protect one of Pablo Escobar's business associates. The job provided decent pay, plenty of leisure time and a chance to pursue a lucrative career in drug trafficking. It also made Gilberto lots of enemies.

He survived several gun battles with rival gangs and began to accumulate the usual perks of his profession: fine clothes, attractive girlfriends, a high-performance motorcycle. The motorcycle was his downfall. He discovered it one Saturday morning in the possession of a rival gang member, who claimed it for his own. A heated argument ensued in which Gilberto pointedly predicted that his rival would be dead by Sunday. His prediction proved true.

Gilberto did not do the killing himself, but he knew that the dead man's friends suspected him of it. He decided to strike them before they could retaliate. At 10.30 one night, he spotted one of the fellows involved in the motorcycle dispute standing on a pavement in Aranjuez. Gilberto walked once around the block to ensure that no police were about, approached the boy from behind and shot him in the head with a .38 calibre revolver.

To his surprise, police officers arrived at his home early the next morning and arrested him for the murder. Unknown to Gilberto, the victim had been standing in front of his own house. His mother and brother had witnessed the murder and identified Gilberto as the assailant. A judge sentenced him to 27 years for the homicide.

A few weeks later he found himself sitting in a Bellavista patio, cradling a knife in his hand and preparing to kill himself. At that moment, Gilberto heard an unfamiliar voice speak a phrase he had never before heard in his life.

'God bless you.'

Gilberto looked up into the smiling face of José Giraldo.

'What did you say?'

'God bless you.' José repeated. 'Did you know he has a purpose for your life?'

'What could that be?'

'He wants you to repent and give your life to him.'

Gilberto asked José what exactly he meant by that.

'I was a *sicario* myself once and God changed me,' he said. 'If God could change my life, he can change yours as well.'

José talked on and Gilberto listened. He forgot about suicide and started considering the possibility of a change in his life. José asked to visit him again in the cell block. After several more visits, Gilberto accepted José's invitation to attend a service in the evangelical chapel. There he heard more about God's plan for his life.

Gilberto endured the taunts of his fellow inmates when he began attending the meetings regularly. 'That Oscar Osorio is a buffoon and he will make a buffoon out of you,' they told him. When they learned Gilberto had prayed the prayer of faith to accept Christ, they taunted him the more. 'Oh, so now you're a repented *sicario*! Until it gets you out of jail, anyway. Then you'll go back to killing, you'll see.'

José Giraldo gave Gilberto a Bible. Because of the taunts, he carried it under his coat when walking through the cell block on his way to the chapel. Then one day, he read Mark 8.38: 'Whoever is ashamed of me and my words in this adulterous and sinful generation, of him will the Son of man also be ashamed, when he comes in the glory of his Father with the holy angels.' The text put Gilberto to thinking. I used to carry a gun and it never bothered me, he said to himself. Why should it bother me now to carry the Word of God? From then on, he carried his Bible in full view. When the other inmates taunted him, he said simply, 'God is helping me. He is the only one who could help me.'

One day Gilberto was walking through Bellavista and encountered a pair of *sicarios* known as the 'Panas'. The two were bitter enemies of his from Aranjuez.

'God bless you,' he said. The Panas glared at him. Gilberto spoke softly. 'I want to ask you to forgive me for trying to kill you that time on the street.'

One of the Panas snatched his Bible away. 'Next time I see you on the street, I'm going to kill you,' he snapped. 'You think this Bible is going to stop the bullets?'

Gilberto looked the angry man in the eye. 'If God wants, he

will protect me. But if not, it doesn't matter. This Bible has power. It changed my life and it can change yours.'

The two Panas glanced at each other. The one who had taken Gilberto's Bible wordlessly handed it back to him.

Over the next few weeks Gilberto told the two Panas more about the change God had made in his life. Eventually they both prayed the prayer of faith and God changed their lives as well. A year later, the Panas were released from prison and promptly resigned from the *sicario* profession. One took a job driving a taxi to support his family and began attending an evangelical church in Medellín. The other became a minister in the evangelical church.

The same year the Panas left Bellavista, Gilberto Paez enrolled in the Bible Institute. Midway through his studies he received a transfer to Villa Hermosa Prison in Cali. The law of the blade still ruled that jail, as it had ruled Bellavista in times past. *Sicarios* killed for trivial offences. One inmate died for failing to flush a toilet after using it, another for aimlessly kicking a garbage can in a prison corridor. Nearly every one of the 1,500 inmates in Villa Hermosa carried a weapon for protection, except Gilberto Paez. He considered that a cowardly act for a man who was looking forward to eternal life.

Gilberto did carry his Bible. Three times Gilberto's Bible was stolen from him. Each time he prayed and asked God to return the book, undamaged. Three times God answered his prayer and the Bible was returned. Gilberto considered that a miracle. He witnessed other miracles in that jail. On some occasions, knife fights erupted while Gilberto preached the gospel to groups of inmates in the prison patio. However, in the 19 months he preached in Villa Hermosa, Gilberto suffered not so much as a scratch. By the time he left Cali to return to Bellavista, a greater miracle had taken place. Forty-five inmates in Villa Hermosa had prayed the prayer of faith to accept Christ.

Gilberto Paez continues preaching the gospel in prison. 'I'm not worried about spending 27 years in jail, but I am worried about offending God,' he tells fellow inmates. Meanwhile, he is completing a theological degree in the Bellavista Bible

Institute. When released, he plans to return to Aranjuez to preach the gospel there.

'I'd like to talk with the boys in the gangs about the God that transformed my life. A lot of them have heard that I accepted Christ, but they don't believe it. To them it's inconceivable that a *sicario* would surrender his life to God.'

Someone pointed out to Gilberto that his life would be in danger if he went back to live in his old neighbourhood. 'No, not really,' he said softly. 'Most of my enemies are dead by now.'

Most, but not all. Some now carry Bibles.

8

New Life Outside the Walls

Adán Colorado gave Oscar Osorio the idea for the New Life Post Penal Centre one June day in 1987. The two men chanced to meet one another on a Medellín street a few days after Colorado's early release from Bellavista.

'What in the world are you doing out of prison?' Oscar asked Adán, surprised by his unexpected parole.

'Living with my sister and looking for a job,' Adán replied.

'Any luck?'

'No, not yet. You know how difficult it is for an ex-offender to find work.'

Oscar did know. 'How long do you plan to be at your sister's?'

Adán frowned. 'I need to find another place soon. It's not a good situation for her and the family.'

Oscar understood that, too. 'Why don't you come and stay with Carmenza and me?' he offered. 'At least, until the Lord shows you the next step.'

Colorado accepted the invitation and moved into the Osorios' modest apartment. From then on, he spent little time looking for employment. He spent most of his time with Oscar inside Bellavista teaching inmates the basics of Christian discipleship. Nearly a year after his release, Colorado still had not found a job. But he did discover the next step the Lord had for him: rehabilitating drug addicts. Adán and Horacio Morales, the same Horacio who painted the words of Matthew 11.28 on the wall in Cell Block Four, established the Rehoboth Jireh Rehabilitation Centre to treat substance abusers.

Adán was not the only ex-offender to share the Osorios' modest apartment upon leaving Bellavista. Carmenza never knew when a stranger or two might be moving into the spare room, but she never protested. Once, however, Carmenza did protest when Oscar gave away their rent money to a destitute ex-offender he chanced to meet on the street.

Oscar did that because he understood, as few people could, the desperate situation men confronted once released from prison. Many were homeless, penniless and friendless. The least he could do as their brother in the Lord was to provide them room and board until they could provide for themselves. But he also realized that the arrangement was stressful for his family, especially after the birth of Juliana.

Oscar and Carmenza began to pray about the dilemma and the Lord provided a solution. Oscar learned that a cousin of his had a room for rent in a shabby tenement six blocks from the Osorios' apartment. The place was a known haunt of *sicarios* and drug addicts; an uncle of Oscar's was murdered on the property by one of the delinquents. Knowing that his cousin dealt with dangerous clientele, Oscar assumed that he would accept ex-offenders as tenants. He did. Oscar paid him 35,000 pesos to rent the room and moved his house guests over there.

Oscar continued teaching them the basics of Christian discipleship. That project involved arriving at the rented room at 5 a.m. to spend time in prayer, singing and Bible study.

Oscar believed he could refurbish the shabby tenement to provide residential quarters and workshops for ex-offenders. One morning he told the men living in the rented room about his idea. 'The Bible says in Joshua 1:3, "Every place that the sole of your foot will tread upon I have given to you,"' he said. 'Let's go and do some treading.' He led the men out of the door and around the building, treading and singing and praying.

Three months later, God answered their prayers. Oscar's cousin offered to sell him the building. Actually, it made good business sense. His other tenants, disturbed by Oscar's early morning treading and singing and praying, one by one had vacated their rooms. No other buyers were interested in the run-down real estate and the price was right. A retired Medellín police officer heard about Oscar's plan to use the tenement building as a halfway house for ex-offenders and donated $6,000 to make the purchase.

Oscar renovated two downstairs rooms into a kitchen and chapel. The rest of the building provided sleeping quarters for former Bellavista inmates. Any of them who needed a roof could live there if they agreed to obey the strict house rules: no drugs, alcohol or extra-marital sex; lots of daily Bible study, work and prayer. Oscar gave it the name 'New Life Post Penal Centre' to reflect the radical transformation God had accomplished in the lives of the *sicarios* and drug addicts who lived there. The title also alerted the neighbours that, even though the tenement house would continue to house a dangerous clientele, it, too, had undergone a radical transformation.

Medellín 1990–97

Like Adán Colorado, Papa Pino was released early from Bellavista with no particular plans. Unlike Adán, he could not live with family, even temporarily. Pino's foul mouth had long alienated him from his numerous relatives. For two years he worked as a locksmith – an honest one – until accepting an invitation to move to the Christian Therapeutic Community in Bogotá, a centre that reclaimed drug addicts and alcoholics. For the next five years, it was Papa Pino's task to locate street people and coax them off their cardboard sheets and into the rehabilitation centre. If they agreed to undergo therapy, Pino burned their grimy clothes, deloused their greasy hair and bathed their gaunt bodies. He also helped to keep the clients properly fed, clothed and sober.

Papa Pino liked the work and would probably have lived out the remainder of his days at the Christian Therapeutic Community, except that he began to read unsettling verses in his Bible. The texts seemed to point him back to Medellín.

I opened my Bible one day and saw Genesis 28.15, where God says, 'I am with you and will keep you wherever you go, and will bring you back to this land.' That had an impact on me. I talked with my pastors and they told me it was

quite mysterious. So I fasted a week and looked at the Word
again. This time it was Jeremiah 24.5–6: 'Like these good
figs, so I will regard as good the exiles from Judah, whom I
have sent away from this place to the land of the
Chaldeans. I will set my eyes upon them for good, and I will
bring them back to this land.'

I was at a farm in the country. About that time, a letter
arrived from my pastor. It said to meditate on the verses I
found in the Bible and make my decision accordingly. So I
said, 'Well, Lord, I'm going to look at the Word one last
time. The Bible fell open at Luke 6.46, 'Why do you call me
"Lord, Lord" and not do what I tell you?' I started to cry. The
only thing to do was take the bus back to Medellín.

When I arrived, I called Pastor Oscar and asked if I could
stay at the post penal centre. 'Sure, why not?' he said. Three
months after I moved in, the leaders there asked me to
become director.

Oscar arranged for Pino to prepare private quarters for
himself in a six-by-three-metre room above the bath house
and gave him charge over cooking, cleaning and enforcing the
house rules. Thus at a time in life when most men retire,
Gerardo found himself undertaking paternal responsibilities.
Papa Pino had inherited a surrogate family. Finally he merited
the nickname Bellavista inmates had given him years before.

*   *   *

Like most residents at the post penal centre, Román Giraldo
occasionally narrates his personal history at local evangelical
churches. He tells his audiences, honestly, that he is a thief. He
used to peddle stolen auto parts to support his alcohol abuse.
However, his thieving could not keep pace with his drinking,
and he looked for other ways to get cash. Alcohol never drove
him to commit murder, although he once earned liquor
money for beating up an old woman who annoyed her neighbour. A brother-in-law sent him extra cash from the United
States, but even that did not suffice to satisfy his craving for
booze. Román was sinking into dereliction.

When his wife left him, he started attending an evangelical church with his sister. He kept stealing, as well. He admits he believed in God, but simply was not prepared to obey him. Román eventually ended up in Bellavista Jail, he believes, for the same reason Jonah ended up in the belly of a fish.

'God put me there to learn the truth.'

Confined to Cell Block Eight, Román met Orlando Taborda. Orlando told him Jesus loved him and had great plans for his life. Later Román met José Giraldo, Oscar Osorio and Jeannine Brabon, who also told him that Jesus had plans for his life. Finally he told them he was tired of sin and was going to change. He did.

Román later explained the change, as he understood it. 'There is a contrast between believing in God and obeying him. A guerrilla may believe in God, but go on killing. What I want to do is obey God. Get away from sin, from self-indulgence, from pride. I ask him every day to let me die to the world, to help me know better his purposes and obey his statutes.'

Román remained in prison long enough to graduate from Bellavista Bible Institute with the first-year class. After his release from jail, he worked as a volunteer on the Prison Fellowship staff and moved into New Life Post Penal Centre. Hyperactive by nature, Román took to preaching on streets and buses, belting out his message through a most prized possession, a megaphone given him by a man who heard him narrate his personal history at a local evangelical church.

'Once a thief, always a thief,' Román says to his audiences. 'Today I go on stealing . . . souls for Jesus!'

* * *

Jaiber Mosquera is a jovial, 29-year-old black man who survived the deadly riots inside Bellavista. He has proof of that: a scar running from abdomen to sternum, the result of a knife attack in March 1990. Using a common tactic among Medellín *sicarios*, Jaiber's assailant smeared the blade with human faeces before cutting him open. Assassins reckon that if the victim survives the initial stabbing, peritonitis will set in and kill him later. To his credit, Jaiber survived both the initial attack and the subsequent peritonitis, but blames the injury for his chronic health problems. To this day, he suffers from anaemia and recurrent bouts of dysentery.

Arrested in September 1986 and charged with armed robbery and car theft, Mosquera served 8 years, 2 months and 11 days of his original 42-year sentence. While in prison, he heard the gospel from Oscar Osorio, Jeannine Brabon and other believers. Like Román Giraldo, he believed in God but refused to obey him.

I ridiculed the gospel. I attended chapel to jeer. I even did work there so I could receive a New Testament. Later I went back to the cell and used its pages to smoke *bazuco*. When a brother greeted me, I would say, 'Yeah, God bless you, man,' but in jest. That's how I was.

When I left jail, I faced a desperate time. Some fellows were looking to kill me because of some, ah, delicate problems I was having. I went to the post penal centre seeking refuge. I planned to stay out of sight for a while, fatten myself up and return to the street. I never considered accepting Christ. I did not read the Bible. Pastor Oscar gave me counsel, but it made me angry. I had a lousy attitude. In fact, three days after arriving at the centre, I slipped out to smoke *bazuco*.

Next day Román Giraldo came up and said to me: 'You left this place last night to go and smoke *bazuco*. My spirit discerned it. Let's see, show me your tongue.'

I said to myself, this fellow must know something. I started taking things seriously. That's how I came to Christ. A week later, I prayed the prayer of faith. I gave myself completely to the Lord. I began reading the Bible and Jesus started giving me fruit. I felt different, like another man.

My family didn't care one bit for me, because I had treated them so poorly. Once I tried to kill my dad. After two months in the post penal centre, I went home. Everybody was startled by the new face they saw and none of them, beginning with my dad, could believe the change in me. We talked and I asked his forgiveness. Dad forgave me and I wept for joy.

Now I'm studying at the Bible Institute and working as a volunteer with Prison Fellowship and with the Villa Boston Evangelical Church. It's my task to escort ex-offenders to judicial hearings. I preach the gospel to the judges. I give my testimony on the city buses. I'm not ashamed of the gospel because it's a living word. My greatest desire is to be a pastor.

To folk in this world, my brothers and I in the post penal centre are nothing but human trash. Nevertheless, God took us and, look, today we're new men.

*   *   *

Daily life at the post penal centre follows a simple routine. After morning worship and breakfast, the inmates leave for Bellavista to clean offices in the administration building or paint prison walls. Once Oscar directed them to refurbish the office of Bellavista's Roman Catholic chaplain, a goodwill gesture that marked the end of competition and the beginning of cooperation between Protestant and Catholic prison staff. When Prison Fellowship commenced working in Buen Pastor Women's Prison, Oscar discovered more maintenance needs there. New Life interns remodelled the dismal cells in the jail's solitary confinement block and installed a seamstress shop so that prisoners could learn a new trade and earn a small income.

Post penal residents dedicate their afternoons to learning new trades themselves. Some work in the centre's small carpentry shop, others pursue part-time employment in local businesses, a few coach football teams sponsored by Mark Wittig's Christian sports club. On weekends, many preach or teach Sunday school in local evangelical churches.

Not all New Life Centre residents are men. At least one family has made its home in the tenement house. When José Giraldo regained his liberty, he moved into a room there with Luz Dary and five-year-old Daniel. The following year, José enrolled in the Autonomous University of Medellín to study Educational Sciences. He is the first ex-offender from Prison Fellowship of Antioquia to enter university, and his colleagues are justifiably proud of him. For his part, Jose is proud that, in his first semester in college, he was able to lead his philosophy professor to the feet of Jesus.

Victor Correa, the Giraldo family's neighbour at the post penal centre, was pursuing university studies himself at one time. He failed to complete his degree, however, because he was jailed in Bellavista on six counts of homicide, kidnap, extortion and terrorism. No serious college student commits such crimes, of course, if he hopes to graduate. But Victor had no choice. Robbery, kidnapping and extortion provided the scholarship that paid his university studies.

Correa grew up in the Medellín borough known as Santa Rosa de Osos, a neighbourhood that registered one to three homicides each day. While in his teens, Victor realized he could easily become a homicide statistic himself. He joined an armed gang to secure access to weapons, hoping to defend his life. The plan worked for a time, but eventually Victor's gang became embroiled in conflicts with rival gangs and local police. The young man sought another avenue of survival.

A band of urban guerrillas known as the Camilista Union for National Liberation (UCLN is the Spanish acronym) learned of Victor's plight. UCLN leaders approached him with an offer he could not refuse. In exchange for his participation in bank robberies, kidnappings and hijackings, activities that financed the UCLN, the guerrillas would pay Victor's tuition at university. UCLN leaders explained that they were interested in training capable young men for professional careers so that one day they could serve the organization more effectively. Victor was eager to pursue a professional career so that one day he could escape the violence of Santa Rosa de Osos.

He was on the professional track until, at the age of 18, he was seriously wounded in a gun battle. Three months later police raided the hiding-place where he was convalescing and arrested him. He spent the next two and a half years in Bellavista Jail, awaiting trial and dreading a conviction that could bring him a maximum sentence of 160 years.

While he waited, Victor met two inmates who altered the course of his life. One was José Giraldo, who told Victor that God had important plans for his life. Eight months after arriving at Bellavista, Victor prayed the prayer of faith and accepted Jesus. He lived in Cell Block Four, where he met the other inmate who altered the course of his life, Jorge Luis Gonzalez. Like Victor, Jorge Luis had been a guerrilla before his arrest. He had also prayed the prayer of faith at the urging of José Giraldo. Victor learned many of the basics of Christian discipleship from Jorge Luis, who pastored the group of believers in Cell Block Four. When Jorge Luis was released from prison, he turned his pastoral duties over to Victor.

Victor's trial failed to produce a conviction, and he was released. For a year afterwards, he worked as a vegetable merchant in the Menorista Plaza. One day Oscar Osorio told him he should start listening to the Lord. 'God has given you aptitude and training,' Oscar said. 'Come and work with us in the prison ministry.' Victor prayed and listened to the Lord and consulted Christian friends and listened some more. Eventually he concluded that God was indeed calling him into the ministry. He enrolled in the Biblical Seminary of Colombia and moved into New Life Post Penal Centre.

'I resigned my job to serve the Lord,' Victor explains, 'and I do what I do for God wholeheartedly. I haven't a peso to my name, but I have God, which is the important thing.'

He also has Laura, a Medellín girl who prayed the prayer of faith with Victor after he told her about the plans God had for her life. They are thinking of marrying some day but have not made a final decision as yet. Meanwhile, they are praying and listening to the Lord and waiting for him to show them the next step.

*   *   *

Daniel Murillo is living proof that Medellín girls feel a strong attraction to *sicarios*. By the time he turned 30, Murillo had fathered three children, all by different mothers. He does not live with any of the women, however. His present address is New Life Post Penal Centre.

I come from a very honest, hard-working home. I have an excellent mother, an excellent father. Father is a welder by trade. He is quite proud of my brothers and sisters who have made professional careers.

A time came when my father suffered disappointment. He was too old to work and almost unable to see from years of welding. Things at home got very bad financially. My dad started drinking heavily. My grandmother was aware of the unpleasant situation and decided to enrol me in a school in another part of the city. It took two hours to get there from my neighbourhood. After a while, I asked grandfather to give me a motorcycle to travel to and from school. I was 14 years old at the time.

We would leave school on the motorbike and head for La Tinajita Park. That field is where my criminal life began. I liked to practise pirouettes on the motorbike. I learned to do circles on one wheel. Once a couple of fellows drove up in a car and watched me doing the turns. Afterwards they offered me a job.

'If you kill this fellow for us, we'll give you 500,000 pesos,' they said. 'We will loan you the weapon. You handle that bike well. You won't have any problem killing him. The police won't catch you. We have it all planned.'

I said to myself, '500,000 pesos is a lot of money. With that I could put a new roof on the house.' It seemed easy enough. So I murdered the fellow. His was the first life I took. I got the money and fixed up the house a bit.

It seemed that killing another person was quite simple. You only had to point the gun at his head and fire. It earned you a lot of money in a matter of seconds. But at night, those few seconds that I managed to see the face of the dead man came back to haunt me. Every detail of the person saturated my memory. I started using marijuana and alcohol so that I could, in some measure, forget that person's face.

Four months later, the two men returned. They said I did good work and offered me another job. I was to murder a man in El Poblado. That one was hard for me because I couldn't shoot him. The police were conducting an investigation nearby, so I couldn't make noise firing a gun. I had to stab him to death with a blade. It was a difficult death, but I did it.

It was okay for me to kill mafiosi because I resented them. I knew they trafficked in drugs and that those drugs killed a lot of young people. I always tried to respect the lives of children, the elderly and women. Sometimes I loaned my motorbike or my gun to take the life of an older person, but I was not capable of killing them myself. I had principles. But if it were a mafioso, no problem.

We formed a gang called 'Los Magnificos'. We were 100 members and we got ourselves into problems with another gang of 100 members. It got to the point that the other boys were killing us off because they had better motorbikes and cars.

Our dream was to work for Pablo Escobar. He was a powerful man, the toughest in town. Pablo had a gold christ implanted in his right shoulder. We said, 'Look, every day they're killing more of us. Let's do what Pablo Escobar did and implant one or two gold christs in our bodies to make ourselves bulletproof.'

Seven of us from the gang went to a surgeon and asked if he could implant the christs. He said, 'Sure, it will cost you 80,000 pesos for each christ. I'll insert one in your trigger finger and another on the left side, over your heart.'

We bought the gold christs from a jeweller. But when we returned to the surgeon, we didn't have enough money to do the implants. He knew who I was, so he said, 'I will make you a proposal. There is this old lady who has been bothering me. If you kill her for me, I'll implant the christs in all seven of you at no charge.'

I said, 'Great. Show us the old lady.'

He pointed her out to us and, a week later, we murdered her.

It was only some time later that we found out that the lady was, in fact, the surgeon's wife. He had her murdered so he could take up with a 16-year-old girl from his neighbourhood. Discovering that the woman we killed was his wife made it tough for us to go and have the christs implanted. We said to each other, 'What happens if the gentleman has regrets and says, "You boys murdered my wife!" Maybe he will plant the scalpel in our hearts.'

The doctor performed the first surgery on my trigger finger. Later, when he was about to implant the christ above my heart, I got quite nervous. But everything went well. The surgeon told us he was very happy with the work we did for him.

I personally have killed at least nine people. It is difficult to give exact figures because we were having conflicts with the other gang. Some nights six, eight or ten fellows died, we never knew how many. I was a gang boss by then. I didn't go out to do the killing myself, but I did send others.

I was arrested and jailed ten times. Once I went to Bellavista for attempted homicide. I put some bullets in a fellow and they caught me two blocks away on the motorbike with the weapon and a bulletproof vest. I told them I hadn't shot the man, that I was simply a bodyguard. The police took 18 months to do a ballistics test, but were never able to prove anything.

Meanwhile, I spent the time in jail. I said to myself that it would be better to take my own life. But I was a coward, unable to kill myself. Pastor Oscar Osorio used to say to me that Christ loved me, that he had great plans for my life. Every time he came by the cell, I would say, 'Here comes that midget again to torment me.' He would say, 'Daniel, my man, Christ loves you in spite of everything.' I was not receptive. The 18 months passed and I left prison. I managed to acquire a house, a car, one or two machine guns – in other words, everything I ever wanted. That was when I began to see that my life was miserable and empty. A son was born to me. I looked at my precious little boy and said, 'My God, if they take this child away from me, it would be like taking my own life.' I had taken the lives of others who had fathers and mothers of their own. In that moment I was able to visualize just where my life was heading.

In July 1994, I went back to jail. For four months, Oscar

preached to me there in the prison. When he came by, he would tear a page out of his Bible and slip it under my cell door. He said, 'Friend, Jesus loves you.' I would answer, 'If he loved me, I wouldn't be in this prison.' I started to read the pages of the Bible. The fact that Oscar would trouble himself to ruin his Bible to slip me a page under the cell door made a great impression on me. One day he said, 'Friend, there are two people interested in your heart: Jesus Christ and myself.' I said, 'Is that so?' He said, 'That's right. Make up your mind to wash yourself in the blood of Christ.'

I wondered, how do you wash in the blood of Christ? I was so ignorant I thought I should have to dump a bucket of blood over me. I was puzzled. One day I went and told the pastor about my confusion. He said, 'Daniel, get on your knees and humble yourself and accept the Lord into your heart. Ask him to forgive your sins.' I said, 'Pastor, can the Lord forgive every sin I have committed?' He said, 'Of course he can forgive you. We have a God who's alive, all-powerful. He is a God who changes everything.'

I knelt and started to cry. I was completely broken. I tried to stop crying, but I couldn't. That night I slept well and woke up the next day at peace, as if the Lord had taken an enormous weight off me. The peace I have now is the kind I had as a child playing in the street, the peace the devil took away.

Here in the post penal centre we have sources of employment. We go to the prisons to work. It's dangerous if we have no job, no means of support. We could return to the old criminal life. Like my father, I know welding. He taught me to build doors, windows, railings. But when you go to prison they issue you a life file. It makes it difficult for an ex-offender to find employment. And if we have no source of income, it's easy to fall back into the old ways. We love the Lord, but our children need clothing and a roof.

I'd like the Lord to send me a woman who fears him. I want to marry a servant of God. My home will be a Christian home. I want my children to grow up to be humble before God.

Once they gave me permission to leave the post penal centre and spend time at home. The neighbours were surprised by the change in me and asked, 'Friend, aren't you afraid to hang around here since you left so many enemies?' I said, 'The Lord restored peace to my life. I don't fear *sicarios* or gangs anymore. I fear only God.'

*   *   *

The surrogate family at the post penal centre that Papa Pino inherited included one genuine blood relative. Nelson Ibarra, the son of Gerardo's sister, Margarita, was a bricklayer and *bazuco* addict. As a child, Nelson learned that his mother and other kin shunned his uncle Gerardo for his foul mouth and his criminal exploits. As an adult, Nelson shared the family's bewilderment when Uncle Gerardo, newly released from Bellavista, began talking to them incessantly about Jesus and urging them to pray the prayer of faith.

Nelson himself spent time in jail for dealing *bazuco*. He was incarcerated only a few months, however. He earned a reduction of sentence for teaching literacy classes to inmates who wanted to rehabilitate themselves. Unfortunately, Nelson failed to rehabilitate himself and returned to his cocaine addiction upon release. One day he awoke from a three-day, *bazuco*-induced stupor and found himself in a grimy coke house. When his head cleared, he realized he had hit rock bottom. He knew the only person who could possibly help him was his uncle Gerardo. Nelson asked his mother Margarita to take him to the post penal centre in Medellín to visit Papa Pino.

Nelson listened once again to Gerardo explain the gospel and prayed for the faith to accept Christ. Not wishing this time to fail at rehabilitating himself, Nelson moved into the New Life Centre to help his uncle with the cooking and cleaning and to participate in the daily routine of prayer, work, worship and study.

For his part, Papa Pino has determined to live at the post penal centre indefinitely, although he does have other options.

He could live with relatives if he wanted. Several members of his extended family, about thirty at last count, have prayed the prayer of faith to accept Jesus Christ. Most of them made that decision after observing the dramatic change in Pino's life and manners.

'They used to be frightened of me because of my language, but now they embrace me,' Gerardo says. 'These days I can't speak, or even recall, the bad words.'

As yet, Papa Pino has not accepted the invitations he has received from several members of his extended family to move in with them. Privately, he confides that he hopes to marry some day and start a family of his own, if he can find a nice, Christian girl. But should he not, he is content to live out his days in the six-by-three-metre room above the bath house at the New Life Post Penal Centre and be a surrogate father to the ex-offenders who come there to wait for the Lord to show them the next step.

9

Martyrs

Jorge Luis Gonzalez was serving time in Bellavista when he learned of the deaths of two American missionaries, Steve Welsh and Timothy Van Dyke. The Revolutionary Armed Forces of Colombia, commonly known as the FARC, kidnapped the two men from a boarding school for missionary children near Villavicencio and held them for 18 months. One day in June 1995, a Colombian army patrol closed in on the guerrillas and shooting started. When it ended, the guerrillas had escaped, but Welsh and Van Dyke had not. The FARC commander executed the two men before fleeing into the bush.

The murders saddened Jorge, himself a former commander of the Fifth Front of the FARC. Gonzalez had hoped to negotiate the missionaries' release after completing his jail term. Six months earlier, he had written to the hostages' families outlining his plan.

'I offer a breath of encouragement on your behalf,' the letter said. 'As soon as I regain my freedom, if God permits I hope to succeed in locating the hostages. The organization that is holding them respects human rights. I used to belong to the same organization. Dear families, not a day passes in which I do not pray for them and for the welfare of you all.'

Steve Welsh and Timothy Van Dyke died despite Jorge's prayers. The young man grappled with disillusionment. Why had God permitted it? He certainly had the power to save their lives. He had saved others. How could he allow two innocent missionaries to go to their deaths, leaving wives and children behind? Eventually Jorge reached his own conclusion about the puzzle and wrote about it in another letter.

14 June, 1995

Dear Mother, Jeannine Brabon,

Today more than ever, I recognize that the battle is not against flesh and blood, but against the principalities of darkness. We must put on the full armour of God and cover ourselves to face the battle.

In these moments, I have been feeling the weight of the prison bars and have told God to take my entire life. I have understood that God has not given us a spirit of cowardliness, but of power, love and self-control. Although it costs to follow Christ, I have decided to give my life for his Word and carry it everywhere, so that everyone who is living without him might know him and honour him as the only God.

Jorge had made a sacred promise. Yet, it is not an uncommon promise. Many Christians make the same promise at one time or another, whether they intend to keep it or not. One thing was certain about Jorge Luis Gonzalez, however. He kept his promises.

*   *   *

Jorge Luis had spent most of his life in the town of Valencia on the torrid Caribbean coast. Bananas grow well in Valencia's steamy climate. In the 1960s, large plantations dedicated to fruit exports thrived there. In the 1970s, exploitation of the peasants who worked the large plantations gave rise to farmers' unions. The unions allied themselves with guerrilla groups like the FARC to pressure plantation owners for better wages and working conditions. In the 1980s, plantation owners allied themselves with drug traffickers to form paramilitary death squads that punished the unions and guerrilla groups for pressuring them. Kidnap, murder and other atrocities multiplied as each side vied for supremacy. The temperature of Valencia's torrid climate rose even higher.

Jorge was raised in Valencia by his grandmother. He never knew his mother, who died when he was an infant. She would have been proud of her son. He excelled in his studies,

especially mechanical drawing, digital electronics and accounting. He formed a musical band that performed folk songs for
weddings and fiestas. While still in his twenties, he ran for city
council on the Liberal Majority ticket and won.

While still in his teens, Jorge had joined the FARC, and he
eventually rose to the rank of commander. The position
brought with it significant personal risk. Once, his folk band
had just finished performing at a rural fiesta when heavily
armed men appeared and forced Jorge into the jungle. They
accused him of being a spy and prepared to shoot him. The
experience so frightened him that he would not talk about it
afterwards. He only remembered asking God to spare his life,
and he did. Several years later, a Colombian army unit arrested
him on suspicion of terrorism and tried to torture a confession
out of him. They did not succeed. Jorge would not talk about
that experience either, except to say that God spared his life
once again.

One day his guerrilla group learned of Colombian army
movements in a rural area near Valencia. Jorge ordered the
road to be mined. His associates demurred, complaining that
the job was too dangerous. So Jorge mounted a horse and
went to do it himself. The squad of soldiers he intended to
blow up arrived at the site before him and caught Jorge with
the incriminating landmine. He expected them to shoot him
on the spot, but they arrested him instead and sent him to jail.
Their magnanimity, Jorge concluded, was another case of God
sparing his life.

At that point in his life, Jorge's belief in God was fairly
vague. On the one hand, he earned spending money making
religious relics and selling them to fellow inmates in the jail.
On the other hand, he did not get on well with his fellow
inmates, fighting 18 skirmishes during his first months among
them. Prison authorities discovered his superior intellect and
employed him as a secretary to prepare legal files. Yet despite
his superior intellect, Jorge was tormented by thoughts of
Satan, the 'Dirty Rat', as he called him.

One night, Jorge had an odd dream. God was telling him

that a strange man would come to help him repent. The time was near. When he told his fellow inmates about the dream, they told him he had gone mad. For some time, Jorge had feared he was going mad but knew he was sane when he dreamed that dream. He got hold of a Bible and started reading it. A few weeks later, prison authorities transferred him to another jail: Bellavista.

Officers assigned Jorge to Cell Block Four, which was reserved for inmates charged with crimes of insurrection. His first day there he took out the Bible and began to read Psalm 23. Another inmate saw him reading and asked Jorge if he was a Christian. 'Of course,' he said.

'So am I,' said the young man, and stuck out his hand. 'We have a group of believers here in the cell block. I'd like you to meet them.'

The Christian inmates welcomed Jorge to their fellowship and asked if he would preach a Bible message the following day. He said he would, though he had no notion at all of what a Bible message was. He talked briefly to the group on the subject of the Antichrist. He could not remember afterwards what he said but did remember being confused and contemplating suicide.

A cell mate invited Jorge to attend a class in human relations taught by José Giraldo in the P3 educational centre. When he learned he could deduct time from his jail term for each day he attended the class, Jorge accepted the invitation.

José Giraldo quickly discovered Jorge's superior intellect. He also perceived that the young man was quite confused about his belief in God.

When we first started the course with him, he came across as quite thick. He didn't believe anything we said about the Lord. He had a very restless mind, probably because he was trying to clear up all the doubts he had.

He was of the Marxist persuasion. He talked a lot about equality. He said religion could never achieve equality for mankind because for all these centuries religion had accomplished nothing. In our day and age, the only thing that could help mankind achieve equality was the revolutionary struggle.

We explained to him that Jesus Christ was concerned about the equality of persons, that in the kingdom of heaven no one person is greater than another. The greatest of all, in fact, is the one who serves others. That caused him to start thinking.

That's when he started to change. Every day he was more interested in reading the Bible as well as other Christian books. When he had doubts, he asked me questions. Lacides Hernandez also talked to him about his doubts.

Jorge talked with Jeannine Brabon about God, as well, and one day prayed the prayer of faith. From then on, his life changed dramatically. His Marxist companions in Cell Block Four were the first to notice. 'What's happened to you?' they asked angrily. 'You don't seem to believe in the revolution any more.'

Jorge responded by inviting them to study Scripture. 'You really ought to read the Bible and see for yourselves what the Lord Jesus says,' he urged. 'Did you know that Jesus advocated a lot of the same ideas about the poor and needy that Marx did? Except that Jesus was 1900 years ahead of Marx.'

'You've been brainwashed!' they sneered.

He smiled. 'Yes, and thank God. My brain needed a good cleaning.'

Jorge began dedicating his superior intellect to learning all he could about the teachings of Jesus. He enrolled in the Bellavista Bible Institute and devoured the theological classics in its small library. José Giraldo appointed him teaching assistant in his P3 human relations class. Jorge began teaching Scripture in Cell Block Four to anyone who would listen. In six months, he convinced 25 fellow insurgents to follow Christ.

A passionate writer, he composed poems to commemorate every important experience in his life. His friends dubbed Jorge the 'Poet of Bellavista'. Lyrics such as 'Farewell to Arms', 'Flowering Anew' and 'Permanent Footprint' marked his spiritual pilgrimage. One doleful ballad recalled the moment in his childhood when he realized he would never meet his own mother. After his conversion, he began sharing his deepest feelings with Jeannine Brabon in letters. The missives were addressed 'To my Beloved Mother, Jeannine'.

When Jorge encountered a gripping quote from one of the theological classics he found in Bellavista's small library, he delighted in sharing it with fellow inmates. One day after reading William Law, he painted a sentence on the back wall of the prison chapel. 'I have made you my only concern, even if it means giving my life for you.' The words were a reminder of Jorge's sacred promise to the Lord.

*   *   *

On 15 January 1996, an officer summoned Jorge Luis from the prison chapel to sign a release document. Freedom caught Jorge completely by surprise. He was even more surprised to learn that the court had absolved him of all past crimes. Exactly 42 months and two weeks after his arrest, Jorge Luis Gonzalez could walk out of Bellavista a free man.

Before doing so, he went back to Cell Block Four and gave away his extra clothing and belongings. He found Victor Correa and asked him to take over leadership of the group of believers that were meeting daily in the patio for prayer and Bible study. At 7.30 that evening, officers ushered him and nine other inmates through the prison's barred doors to freedom.

No one waited at the main gate to greet Jorge because none of his friends knew he was being released. He dialled several phone numbers before reaching Prison Fellowship volunteers, who promised to be there in 25 minutes. The delay gave him time to talk about the gospel with a newly released inmate who was also waiting at the main gate for a ride. When his friends arrived, they found Jorge leading the young man in the prayer of faith.

Jorge moved into the New Life Post Penal Centre and waited for the Lord to show him the next step. He continued studying in the Bible Institute and began preaching on Medellín streets and at the Villa Boston evangelical church. He initiated a Bible study group at a local factory and another in a jail for delinquent police officers. Within three months, he had convinced 20 of the inmates there to follow Christ. In a letter to Jeannine Brabon, he marvelled that God had placed him in favour with men he once had loathed.

Despite his evangelistic successes, Jorge was restless to fulfil a cherished dream: preaching the gospel in his native Valencia. He proposed the venture on numerous occasions to Oscar Osorio and Lacides Hernandez. The two refused to consider it, lecturing Jorge on the dangers. 'The paramilitary squads virtually rule the area,' Oscar told him. 'Your old enemies will shoot you on sight.'

'But imagine the impact my testimony could have on my family and former associates in the guerrilla forces,' Jorge countered. 'They need to hear the gospel and I'm the logical person to take it to them.'

'I'm not afraid of the danger,' he insisted. 'After all, we are covered in the blood of Jesus, aren't we?'

Jorge eventually succeeded in convincing Lacides to take him home. They left Medellín on Palm Sunday and drove to Planeta Rica. That evening, Jorge and Nelson Palacios, a former *sicario* who also found Jesus in Bellavista, shared their testimonies in an evangelical church in Planeta Rica. The congregation responded enthusiastically, embracing the two young ex-offenders like long-lost relatives. Although he still felt some uneasiness, Lacides began to imagine Jorge receiving the same kind of welcome in Valencia.

Lacides had business that kept him in Planeta Rica, so next day he put Jorge and Nelson on the bus to Valencia. Lacides promised to collect his two friends in Valencia the following Saturday. 'We'll see you at my father's house,' a beaming Jorge told him. 'Come prepared for the best food you will ever eat in your life!'

Jorge created no little stir when he arrived at the Gonzalez home later that day. Word quickly spread that he had returned from prison. The first person who came to greet him was his grandmother, her expression a mixture of joy and anxiety. 'Do not leave this house while you are in Valencia,' she cautioned him. 'Maybe they won't find out you've come.' Jorge assured her that he would stay indoors.

Next day, he was too restless to keep his promise. 'Come on, Nelson,' he said to his companion. 'I want to show you around town.'

They got as far as the Presbyterian Church. Jorge struck up a conversation with the pastor, who invited him and Nelson to share their life stories at Wednesday vespers. Jorge eagerly accepted. The ex-guerrilla's testimony created an even greater stir in Valencia. On Thursday morning, Jorge was showing Nelson around town on a bicycle when three fellows summoned him to the kerb. They wanted to know how long Jorge would be in town. A few more days, he said, and told them he had come to Valencia to share the gospel of Jesus. Straight away Jorge began sharing the gospel with them. They listened a bit before interrupting to ask *exactly* how much longer he would be in town.

Their insistence made Nelson uneasy. His uneasiness later intensified when Jorge pointed out four other fellows watching them from the pavement. 'Those are old enemies of mine,' he told Nelson.

'Look, Jorge, I think we must be prudent,' Nelson said. 'I don't think it's wise to stay here. Let's go back to Planeta Rica.'

'Easy, brother,' Jorge said. 'Nothing is going to happen. Don't you believe we are covered by the blood of Jesus?'

Nelson said nothing.

After lunch that day, Nelson was peeling a papaya in the Gonzalez kitchen when five men, heavily armed and hooded, stormed into the house. 'Where is Jorge Luis Gonzalez?' they demanded.

'He's not here. I don't know where he went,' Nelson lied, hoping his friend had escaped over the back wall.

Just then Jorge, in shorts and shirtless, ambled in from the back yard. 'I'm Jorge Luis Gonzalez,' he said.

The masked men shoved Nelson into a chair and forced his head down. They grabbed Jorge by the arms.

'We have a truck waiting outside,' they said. 'You are to come with us.'

'Pardon me, gentlemen, but I'm not going anywhere with you,' Jorge answered.

They pointed their machine guns at him. 'Get in the truck,' they repeated.

'No thank you.'

A scuffle ensued. Nelson could see nothing of what was happening. He heard a short burst of machine gun fire and the thud of a body falling to the floor. The commotion stopped. Nelson held his breath, awaiting the impact of the bullets in his own body. Nothing happened. After several seconds, he raised his head to see what was happening. The masked men were gone. Jorge lay beside him on the kitchen floor in a pool of blood. The Poet of Bellavista was dead.

*   *   *

At 5 o'clock that afternoon, a pallid Nelson Palacios arrived at Planeta Rica to give Lacides Hernandez the news of Jorge's murder. When Lacides had overcome his shock, he offered to return with Nelson to Valencia to bury their friend.

'We can't do that,' Nelson said. 'It's too dangerous. The paramilitary are everywhere.' Instead they telephoned the Gonzalez family to express their condolences and offer what support they could. It was too late to return to Medellín that night, so they rang Jeannine Brabon to tell her the news.

During the rest of that long evening, Lacides listened to Nelson describe Jorge's final days in Valencia. 'He could have escaped, but he knew they would kill the rest of us if he did,' Nelson said. 'You know something. Jorge Luis gave his life for us.'

The truth is, Jorge Luis Gonzalez gave his life for Jesus. His friends in Bellavista realized that immediately when they learned of his death. Someone even mentioned that it was no coincidence that Jorge was buried on Good Friday, the same day Christ sacrificed himself on the cross.

Victor Correa will never forget his friend from Cell Block Four. 'That conviction, that assurance he had in knowing in

whom he had believed was an incentive for me to keep perse-
vering,' the young ex-guerrilla said. 'And of course, there is
that phrase he wrote on a wall in Bellavista. It had a great
impact on me. It says, "If Jesus Christ be God and died for me,
then no sacrifice is too great for me to make for him."'

Jorge had read those words of C. T. Studd in one of the
theological classics he found in Bellavista's small library. They
convey a sacred promise. One thing is certain about Jorge Luis
Gonzalez. He kept his promises.

*   *   *

On 22 July 1992, Pablo Escobar missed an opportunity, perhaps
his final one, for redemption. On that day, Fangio Quiroz
planned to visit Escobar in 'The Cathedral', the drug lord's
private prison. Thirteen months earlier, Escobar had voluntarily
surrendered to the authorities. Under a special arrangement
with the Colombian government, he agreed to submit to justice
provided he could serve his sentence in the luxurious jail he
had built for himself in the town of Envigado, near Medellín.

Fangio Quiroz, a distant relative of Pablo Escobar, wanted to
share the gospel with the boss of the Medellín cartel and invite
him to pray the prayer of faith. But hours before their meeting
was to take place, Escobar's aides telephoned to tell Fangio
that Escobar was unable to see him but would be in touch to
reschedule the interview. What the aids did not tell Fangio
was why their boss could not meet with him. Escobar was
planning his escape from the Cathedral.

The drug lord did indeed escape from his private jail in
Envigado. However, he enjoyed less than 18 months of freedom. The noose Gustavo De Greiff was tightening around
him drew closed on 11 December 1993. A squad of narcotics
officers surrounded Escobar in a Medellín hideout and a sharp
gun battle ensued. The drug lord and his bodyguard slipped
out of a back window and climbed onto the roof, attempting
to escape. They did not.

When news of Escobar's death reached Bogotá, police and
government officials gathered to celebrate the victory.
Reporters telephoned Gustavo De Greiff to ask how he felt

about the success of his relentless pursuit of the drug lord. Colombia's top lawman gave an answer typical of a decent, God-fearing citizen doing his patriotic duty. 'I feel satisfaction and sadness,' the Prosecutor General told them. 'Satisfaction that justice has finally triumphed, sadness at seeing yet another life wasted.'

Pablo Escobar's death saddened Fangio Quiroz, as well. More than most, he understood how tragically the man had wasted life. Fangio had wasted a good chunk of his own life working for Escobar in the Medellín drug cartel.

Fangio had embarked on his criminal career at a tender age, even by Medellín standards. He was 11 years old the first time he attempted murder. His father sent him out with a knife to dispatch a neighbourhood witch who bothered him. The woman escaped the assault. Fangio attributed it to her skill in the black arts. However, few of his future targets would be so fortunate.

Murder was not Fangio's only vice. His father gave him his first drink of *aguardiente* at the age of four. By age 19, he had destroyed his liver and kidneys with drink and drugs. Since he worked for drug traffickers, he could buy *bazuco* whenever he wanted. Before his twentieth birthday, Fangio had drunk so much *aguardiente* and smoked so much *bazuco* that he was nearly dead.

He was hiding out at the home of an aunt after dispatching an enemy of the Medellín cartel when the end came. For a week he had not eaten, living off booze and cocaine. He started vomiting blood and could not muster the strength to get out of bed. He believed he was dying. 'The *sicario* demon is a real strong man,' he later told a friend, 'one that gets inside you to kill. He certainly was inside me.'

Fangio told his aunt he was going to die. 'It's for the best,' he said.

His aunt disagreed. 'Look, if your cousin, who was once so mean, could change, I think you can change, as well.'

Her lecture penetrated the fog in Fangio's brain and renewed his will to live. He heard a supernatural voice telling him to go to Medellín and look for his cousin in an evangelical church. He got out of bed, bathed and ate and took a bus for the city. Fangio arrived there on a Saturday evening and found his way to the church. He enjoyed the singing and the Bible message. Most of all, he enjoyed the peace. He returned the following morning. When the preacher invited anyone who wanted to accept Jesus to come down to the front, Fangio dashed down the aisle.

'That day, the *sicario* demon died in me,' he later told a friend. 'So did the vulgarities, the drugs, the alcohol. The Lord automatically healed my brain and neurons. In that instant, my life changed.'

Fangio's life changed so dramatically that the Central Pan American Church of Medellín hired him as a minister. He met two persons at the church who would cause further changes his life. One was Doris Gomez, whom Fangio started courting the year she graduated from high school. Mrs Gomez counselled her daughter against it. 'That boy has had an evil past,' she warned. 'He destroyed his health with drugs. He is not good husband material.' Doris had her own doubts about Fangio, right up until their wedding day.

'Inside I worried that perhaps my life would not turn out as I hoped,' Doris later confided to a friend. 'I thought that maybe Fangio would abuse me. But it's turned out entirely different than I expected. God has given me so many surprises with this man.'

Oscar Osorio was the other person who would help change Fangio's life. The two were chatting one day at the church when Oscar mentioned his work in Bellavista Jail. Fangio confided a long abiding interest in taking the gospel to men in prison. 'Well, brother,' Oscar said, 'if you'd like to work with us, you are welcome.'

Fangio started praying about the possibility and felt God leading him to resign his position on the Central Pan American Church staff and join Prison Fellowship. Oscar assigned him to work in Cell Block Twelve and in Bellavista's new Maximum Security wing, areas reserved for inmates with a price on their heads. Prison officials confined them there for their own protection. Many of these prisoners had previously worked for drug cartels and had made powerful enemies. Some of those enemies were prepared to pay huge amounts of cash to have them killed. Some of Bellavista's inmates were willing to kill them, for huge amounts of cash, even though it meant wasting their own lives.

*   *   *

Fangio Quiroz chanced to meet an old friend in Cell Block Twelve: Juan Carlos Londoño, alias Juan Caca. The two had known each other during the years they worked together in the Medellín drug cartel. Fangio was delighted to learn that Juan had since received Jesus and renounced what had been his criminal speciality: building car bombs.

'Brother Fangio, if I had only known that Christ was so wonderful,' Juan said, 'I would never have committed all those bombings. To be with Christ is the best thing that I've ever found in my life. It's a shame I didn't follow him sooner.'

Juan Caca started following Christ soon after he and Ñangas were arrested in March 1993. Prison Fellowship volunteers visited him in jail in Bogotá, where he was being held for questioning. They told Juan that Jesus had died for his sins – including the car bombings. That piqued his curiosity and he began reading the Bible. Before the authorities transferred Juan to Bellavista to begin serving his 40-year sentence, he prayed the prayer of faith.

Jan Mario Henao, another old friend who had worked with Londoño in the Medellín cartel and who also had received Jesus since his capture, immediately sensed the change in Juan when the young man arrived at Bellavista.

'When they brought Juan Carlos from Bogotá, I realized he was different. He had changed from being a violent, arrogant man to a humble one. People were watching him closely. He was, after all, a malicious terrorist. But the change in the man's personality was total.'

In October 1994, Oscar Osorio baptized Juan Carlos Londoño in the Bellavista chapel. The act was a public testimony of the change in the young man's life. Juan subsequently enrolled in the Bellavista Bible Institute and began leading worship in the prison chapel. In October 1996, Oscar Osorio officiated at a second public ceremony in the chapel that further attested to the change God had made in Londoño. Juan wed Gloria, his long-time companion and the mother of his three-year-old daughter, Daniela.

Like many Medellín girls, Gloria was attracted to Juan when he was working as a *sicario*. Later when she visited him in prison and he told her of his conversion to Christ, she was sceptical. Juan read to her from the Bible and explained the change that God had made in his life. He told her he was praying that she, too, would receive Jesus. When Gloria finally did, the couple started planning their wedding.

The same day the Londoños were married, Jan Mario Henao wed Liliana, his long-time companion and the mother of his infant daughter, Samantha, in the Bellavista chapel. Jan Mario understood better than most the meaning of a jailhouse wedding in the life of a former *sicario*.

'A *sicario* would never do what we Christians do here in jail – get married, that is,' he explained. 'Know why? Because the *sicario* is arrogant, he wants only the best for himself. To celebrate your wedding in a place like Bellavista, a real dump, well, you have to be a genuine Christian to do that.'

In Juan's case, he had to be genuinely brave, as well. Prison officials warned Londoño that he was taking his life in his hands every time he left the security of Cell Block Twelve to walk through the prison yard to the chapel. They reminded him of his many powerful enemies who would like to see him dead. They also pointed out that there were still some inmates in Bellavista willing to kill him, for the right price. 'I'll take that risk,' Juan told them. 'I used to risk death for criminal causes. I prefer to die for the cause of Christ.'

Six days after his wedding to Gloria, Juan was leaving Cell Block Twelve on his way to the chapel. He spotted Jan Mario Henao across the prison yard and smiled. Jan Mario will never forget what happened next.

'I saw Juan leave his cell block and I waited in the prison yard to meet him. But before he reached me, a fellow with a pistol stepped in front of him. He shot Juan three times in the face.'

Juan fell dead to the ground, still clutching his Bible, still smiling peacefully. Prison guards immediately tackled the assassin, an inmate named Gabriel Rueda Vargas. The officers wrested the weapon from his hand and carried him off to La Guayana.

A stunned Jan Mario struggled with the shock of Londoño's brutal murder. 'His death was hard on me because he and I had shared so much as brothers in the Christian life,' he confided to a friend. 'I loved him very much. At that moment, I was almost at the point of giving up, going back to the world and abandoning the gospel.'

'But I realize that this experience will help me face other, more difficult experiences that are sure to come. Material things pass away but spiritual things last. Juan lives on, only now he lives with an advantage. He made it to the kingdom of heaven before me.'

It was rumoured among Bellavista inmates that Londoño's powerful enemies had paid Rueda Vargas $200,000 dollars for the murder. The motive remained unclear, although it certainly had something to do with the fact that Juan Carlos had once belonged to Pablo Escobar's inner circle. The pinnacle of the cartel hierarchy never knew such things as compassion, pity or pardon.

What is clear is that, for a large sum of money, Rueda Vargas was willing to waste two lives, Londoño's and his own.

But perhaps the lives were not wasted after all. As Jeannine Brabon comforted Gloria Londoño after her husband's funeral, the young widow said, 'It's sad to see him die in this cruel way, but thank God, Juan died in Jesus and not in his life of crime. He planted a wonderful seed in me, the seed of eternal life. I hope to be faithful to plant it in others.'

'Know what?' she added. 'When it's the right moment, I want to give a Bible to the fellow who killed my husband. I don't want his soul to be lost. I know Juan would want the young man to find the same forgiveness he received from God.'

Fangio Quiroz understood, better than most, the forgiveness Juan Carlos Londoño had received. 'You know something, Fangio,' Juan told him at their last meeting in Cell Block Twelve, 'even though I'm in this prison, condemned to 40 years, I'm happy. I know Christ lives in me. That is *real* freedom.'

Then Juan gave Fangio a Bible as a memento of their long friendship. He opened the book to the title page and signed his name before handing it to him.

'Brother Fangio, we belong to Christ,' Juan said, smiling. 'He is the best friend I've ever found. Keep going on with him.'

10

The Lord of Bellavista

People will remember Juan Carlos Londoño for many reasons, perhaps the most remarkable being that his murder was the only violent death recorded inside Bellavista Jail in 1996. The same prison that once claimed 50 lives a month has averaged only one homicide per year since 1990, when Oscar Osorio envisioned God wrapping the jail in his hand and received divine orders to raise white flags and pray. During the same six-year period, Oscar baptized 514 inmates in a makeshift baptistery in the prison chapel. Christian conversions have replaced murders as Bellavista's most impressive statistic.

Colombia's law enforcement community is aware of the change inside the jail. Many find it difficult to believe that an evangelical awakening could pacify the most violent prison in the Western world. Dr Orlando Lopez, Bellavista's vice-governor who directs Industrial and Educational Services in the jail, does not. Lopez has observed the change firsthand.

'Truthfully, the Lord has his hand on Bellavista,' Lopez told a visiting journalist one day in the prison cafeteria. 'The violence here has diminished 90 per cent. This is due to the careful job the prison personnel are doing and to prayer. We have prayer groups in every cell block.'

'People are beginning to comprehend that praying in a cell block is effective. Inmates form a different outlook on life. The religious factor has rehabilitated people. That's where you see the importance of the gospel inside Bellavista Jail. In spite of the fact that this is the most crowded jail in the country, men are changing the way they live.'

'We hope', he added, 'that Bellavista continues to change.'

For seven years, Orlando Lopez has worked in the jail,

making him one of the most senior members of the present administrative staff. Luz Elena Torres, who began her teaching career in La Ladera in 1971, is *the* most senior member of the staff. Like Dr Orlando, she believes prayer can change a prison, even a violent one.

'Bellavista was the worst jail in Colombia,' she told a visiting journalist one day in her prison classroom. 'Inmates killed for a wristwatch or a light bulb. They did not kill me because people were praying for me.'

Luz Elena, a self-described 'Christian of the pew' until 1988, experienced a revival in her own life that inspired her to become part of the evangelical awakening inside the jail.

'A brother named Javier Celis arrived as a Prison Fellowship volunteer. He was to teach third grade in the primary school programme, but he told me he thought he was to teach biblical discipleship. I said I didn't know what biblical discipleship was. He said it was something that revealed the glory of the Lord.'

'Fine,' I said, 'let's do an exchange then. I will teach you what I know about primary education and you teach me to know the Lord better. As Coordinator of the P3 educational centre, I thought it would be good to teach discipleship to the inmates in the jail.'

Oscar Osorio arrived soon afterwards to work towards the same goal that Javier Celis, Luz Elena Torres and other Prison Fellowship volunteers were pursuing. Oscar described that goal to a visitor one day in the prison chapel.

'My vision is to form in all these young men disciples who serve the Lord, so they can succeed in penetrating places of shadow. I want them to be a light there to preach the gospel.'

*   *   *

Picaleña Penitentiary in Ibague, a nine-hour journey from Medellín, is a place of shadow. Among the 1,000 inmates in Picaleña are some of Colombia's most dangerous criminals.

José Amador was seven years old when he witnessed his neighbours murder his father. Amador plotted revenge. He bided his time until he was old enough to join a guerrilla army and learn to handle weapons. Soon after that, several of his neighbours turned up dead. Security forces traced the murders to Amador. He entered jail at the age of 25 on charges of terrorism and subversion against the state. Now 42, Amador has few visitors and few prospects for release.

In 1977, José Claros received a 48-month sentence for misconduct in the military, but his jail term has since stretched to 46 years. Prison psychiatrists have diagnosed Claros as a psychopathic killer. He complains that invisible demons have forced him to kill five fellow inmates. One cell mate died after Claros read a horoscope that warned him 'to beware of the person who sleeps at your side'. 'I said to myself, the fellow in the next bunk must be planning to do me harm,' Claros explained. 'So I killed him before he could kill me.' Claros has spent six of his 20 years behind bars in psychiatric wards.

Ariel Herrera, known throughout the Colombia prison system simply as 'Charli', is serving the longest prison sentence currently on record: 108 years. Charli has spent the past 23 years in jail, giving him more seniority than any Colombian now behind bars. Originally convicted as a teenager on 16 counts of homicide, he has killed 12 men while in jail. But he is not psychopathic.

'One had to kill to conserve one's integrity as a man,' he shrugs. 'At the time I entered prison I was 17 years old and homosexuality was rampant. If you wanted respect, you had either to take others' lives or give up your own.'

Until a year ago, Picaleña authorities took extra precautions to keep bloodshed to a minimum. They segregated guerrilla fighters from *sicarios*, and members of the Cali drug cartel from their Medellín rivals. Still, inmates killed and maimed one another. Guards never allowed inmates from alien cell blocks to mingle in the jail's central corridor because they instinctively attacked one another on sight.

Early in 1994, the authorities transferred Fernando Arroyave from Bellavista to Picaleña. The violence of his new surroundings shocked the policeman-turned-*sicario*-turned-missionary.

'We were all afraid, because this is such a dangerous place,' he told a visiting journalist one day inside Picaleña. 'There are lots of people sentenced to long prison terms here. But because I had received Christ in Medellín, he filled me with confidence.'

'I was like Jonah in the belly of the whale. The prophet renewed himself in there to go back out and preach in obedience the holy calling. God has a purpose in having us pass through places like this, because every believer's mission is to announce the gospel of salvation.'

Fernando met others who had accepted the call to announce the gospel in Picaleña. In 1967, Maria Rodriguez, a member of the Presbyterian church in Ibague, began weekly visits to Ibague's jails to distribute soap, toothbrushes, eye glasses and gospel tracts to the prisoners. Truthfully, Maria had no business becoming a prison evangelist. A single mother – her husband had abandoned the family – she sold homemade pastries to support her 14 children. But Maria once heard that Jesus commanded his followers to visit those in prison, so she did. In 1982, Mrs Rodriguez affiliated her ministry with Prison Fellowship. When she passed away, her daughters Ruth and Gladys, along with a small corps of Ibague ladies, continued her jail ministry. Picaleña inmates know them simply as 'the sisters'.

Two years after Fernando arrived at Picaleña, a team from the New Life Post Penal Centre visited him there. The ex-offenders from Medellín visited the cell blocks, unit by unit, and shared the gospel. By the time they finished, the team had led some 300 Picaleña inmates in the prayer of faith.

When the New Life team returned to Medellín, the fellows presented Jeannine Brabon with an urgent request. 'We have to send a missionary to Picaleña. The believers there need help discipling all those new Christians.'

'Where are we going to find a missionary?' Jeannine asked. 'And how are we going to finance one?'

'Well,' they said, 'the inmates in Bellavista have agreed to raise enough money to support a missionary in Ibague. We are fasting and praying that God will set apart the right person.'

The following month, God set apart Fangio Quiroz and his wife, Doris. The couple moved to Ibague in April with their five-year-old son, Charles Finney, to reinforce the small corps of Prison Fellowship volunteers there. Fangio carried a letter from the National Director General of Prisons authorizing him 'to carry out measures of evangelization of the inmates . . . from Monday to Friday, mornings and afternoons'. Fangio believed that, with the Director General's signed authorization, he would have no problem entering the penitentiary, even if he were a distant relative of Pablo Escobar. He was wrong.

At his first meeting with Imelda Lopez, the new governor of Picaleña, Fangio was denied a prison pass.

'I'm sorry, Pastor Quiroz,' Mrs Lopez told him, 'but we have serious security problems at this facility. Most of our inmates are serving extended terms. They are considered highly dangerous.'

The governor's blunt refusal caught Fangio off guard. He could think of only one thing to say.

'Dr Lopez, the Lord loves you very much. You are valuable to the Lord Jesus.'

The governor stared at Fangio. After several moments, he thought he detected a slight softening in her gaze.

'Yes, . . . well, is there someone in particular you would like to see today?' she asked.

'Fernando Arroyave. Cell Block Two.'

Before the week was out, Imelda Lopez had reconsidered the security risks of allowing Fangio to freely visit the cell blocks. She issued him with a pass allowing him to enter Picaleña any weekday, mornings and afternoons. Fangio started visiting the cell blocks that held the penitentiary's most violent inmates.

'Aren't you afraid to go in there?' the guards asked him. 'You know you could easily get yourself killed.'

'The Lord is with me,' Fangio told them. 'Years ago, he rescued me from a life of crime. I expect he can take care of me in here.'

The Lord did take care of Fangio. Within a year of his arrival, he was meeting with groups of inmates three mornings a week in Picaleña's cell blocks to teach them the basics of Christian discipleship. Every weekend, Fangio, Doris and Charles Finney slept on their kitchen floor, giving up their beds to the wives and children of Picaleña inmates who came from out of town for visiting day.

Within a year of Fangio's arrival, Picaleña had changed dramatically. By then, guards were permitting inmates from alien cell blocks to mingle in the jail's central corridor because they no longer attacked one another on sight. Guerrilla fighters and *sicarios* were working side-by-side in the prison woodshop. Members of the Cali drug cartel were meeting to study the Bible together with their rivals from the Medellín cartel. Prison guards had not registered a single escape attempt in an entire 12-month period, a record for the facility. Picaleña's security problems had dramatically diminished.

Some of Colombia's most dangerous criminals in Picaleña have changed, as well. 'I used to like the ideas of the revolution, but I don't subscribe to them anymore,' José Amador told a visitor one day in the prison woodshop. 'I'm learning the Word of God. The sisters come every other day to visit and we talk about the Word. It gives one strength to go on, day by day, serving the Lord.'

Prison authorities are considering an early release for José Claros. He has not murdered anyone since 1990. Nor has José complained about invisible demons since finding Jesus in a psychiatric ward in Bogotá's La Picota jail.

'I don't believe in horoscopes any more,' Claros said. 'I like to read what the Bible has to say. I'm grateful to Pastor Fangio and all the volunteers of Prison Fellowship who have given me biblical counsel. Now I don't believe in what the devil says, but in what God says.'

Charli found Jesus in 1993 in La Picota prison, through talking with Mrs Esperanza Martinez, a volunteer of the Bogotá Prison Fellowship. Today, the inmate with the most seniority in Colombia's prison system is allowed to walk freely through the central corridor of Picaleña. He carries a big, red Bible under one arm that he uses to teach the basics of Christian discipleship to the 25 inmates in Cell Block Six who have accepted Jesus.

'There was a big change in my life,' Charli says. 'The Lord transformed all the hardness in my heart and started filling me with his holy presence. Formerly, I was known as one of the most dangerous prisoners in the penitentiaries. Now, when they see the change the Lord has made in my life, well, a lot of fellows here in Picaleña come to the feet of Jesus.'

Imelda Lopez credits the volunteers of Prison Fellowship for helping bring about the remarkable change in Picaleña.

'The contribution Fangio Quiroz has given us has been invaluable,' she told a visiting journalist one day in her office. 'You have probably noticed that a large number of inmates are young men with long sentences. They don't have much hope.'

'But suddenly they saw in Fangio a man who escaped from that profound abyss and succeeded in going on. It gives these fellows some hope.'

*   *   *

Oscar Osorio has given hope to hundreds of men behind bars. As much as any other man, he has lived the triumphs and tragedies of the evangelical awakening inside Bellavista Jail. The tragedies have been poignant. Besides Juan Carlos Londoño and Jorge Luis Gonzalez, Oscar lost another good friend and ally in 1996, when assassins murdered Carlos Arturo Rios. Major Rios had gained a reputation for integrity and competence in his two years as Governor of Bellavista.

It is no small miracle that assassins have not murdered Oscar. Threats against his life are so frequent, he can't remember them all. Carmenza Osorio remembers a message left by an anonymous caller on the family's answering machine one day when Juliana was seven. 'You had better take good care of your little girl,' the gruff voice sneered, 'or I just might put a bullet in her.'

Carmenza refuses to be intimidated by her family's enemies. 'Truthfully, even that threat did not upset me, because God has always given me an immense peace,' she says. 'I put my trust in the Lord.'

Jeannine Brabon shares Carmenza's philosophical attitude towards the dangers of working among some of the most dangerous criminals in Medellín. 'Security is not the absence of danger,' Jeannine is often heard to say. 'It is the presence of Jesus.'

Not all the tragedies in Medellín have been violent ones. Orlando Taborda was obliged to resign as assistant pastor of Bellavista Chapel when his marriage collapsed. Abuse and infidelity during his years as a *sicario* had caused deep stress fractures in his relationship with his wife, Beatriz. Although they tried, the couple could not reconcile their differences and eventually divorced. Not wanting to compromise Prison Fellowship's reputation for integrity, Orlando left the staff to accept work as a chauffeur. Today, he declines to preach in public but witnesses privately to friends and associates of the change he underwent when he found Jesus in Bellavista.

Until his untimely death in April 1998, Adán Colorado continued to operate the Rehoboth Jireh Association, the substance abuse treatment programme he established after his release from Bellavista Jail. He was so successful in rehabilitating drug users that he had to expand his operation from one to five treatment centres.

'It's something truly miraculous, what God began to do in that prison,' Colorado said. 'I recall the mercies of God in that place, all the things he did in the lives of so many men, who today are serving in different ministries.'

*   *   *

Several of José Giraldo's former criminal associates, as well as members of his family, have accepted Jesus. The former professor from the P3 educational centre says this has been a great blessing on his life. But José has experienced his share of painful tragedy, as well.

In 1995, they killed my 20-year-old brother, Fernando, on the street. He used drugs. Years ago, the two of us committed robberies together.

I had another brother, Didier, who was 15 years old. I brought him to the feet of Jesus when he visited me in prison.

Didi attended church regularly. When they murdered

Fernando, Didi stole a pistol from the place where my father worked. He told everybody he was going to avenge Fernando's death.

Papa went out and found him shooting target practice. He scolded him and Didi turned over the pistol. That shows me that Didi still feared God and respected his parents. Nevertheless, a month later the same fellows who killed Fernando murdered Didi.

I found out who they were. My old friends told me that, if I wanted to make the arrangements, they would help me kill my brothers' murderers. I said, 'No thanks, I'm not that kind of person any more. I am a son of God and I have forgiven them.'

I am praying for those fellows. Maybe sometime in the future, they will find themselves in jail and I will have an opportunity to speak to them about Christ. My hope is that, although I have lost my brothers, I might gain these other fellows as spiritual brothers.

My dad was a man who enjoyed vigorous health, but the deaths of my two brothers hit him hard. From then on, he could not come to visit me any more in jail because he was so sick. When I left prison in December 1995, Papa was fighting cancer of the pancreas. He was a Christian. I had brought him to the Lord several years before and he had been baptized. He was an active member of the Evangelical Covenant Church. During December and January, I was able to talk with him for hours on end. I could really see Jesus in him, despite the pain and suffering. Papa died 29 January 1996. He was trusting in the resurrection.

I immediately became involved with Prison Fellowship of Antioquia. I work in the jail's maximum security section. The brothers offered me a small room in the post penal centre to live with Luz Dary and José Daniel. I had always wanted to accumulate wealth, but with the gospel, one learns to rejoice in scarcity as well as in abundance. I hope to provide the necessary things for my wife and child, but I no longer care about luxury.

In 1997, I enrolled in the Autonomous University of

Medellín, paying my tuition with 350,000 pesos of bail money the court returned to me. Following the advice of Pastor Oscar and Sister Jeannine, I decided to study Educational Sciences. My goal is to enrich my ministry, to prepare myself to serve the Lord more effectively. In the not-too-distant future, I hope to teach in a secular high school or university. I notice the professors are always trying to pull the rug out from under us Christians, to use their knowledge to rob us of our faith. I want the opportunity to be somebody unique. I would like to pull the rug out from under them.

I'm very concerned for young people. I think youth today are lost. They have no direction. A teacher can be a role model for his students. It gives you a platform to be a good counsellor and thus help them avoid falling into crime.

That is my desire. But I also plan to follow the Lord in the jails. I never want to leave that work.

*   *   *

The spiritual awakening in Bellavista has its share of critics. An anthropologist once conducted a study of Oscar Osorio's ministry and concluded that he had brainwashed the inmates. In September 1994, the scientist's findings were reported in the Medellín daily *El Tiempo*. The article elicited a passionate response from Jorge Luis Gonzalez.

'Oscar has not "brainwashed" us, inducing us to cover up our sins,' wrote the Poet of Bellavista. 'He has never charged one peso for his worthy and marvellous labour. It is no doctrine of fanaticism that he teaches us. We invite you, distinguished journalist sir, to come in person to the Bellavista National Jail and see for yourself that God alone has transformed our old lives.'

'We have a brother who deserves an award and recognition from the Colombian people for the labour which he has conducted,' Jorge Luis concluded. 'I am speaking of Pastor Oscar Osorio Castañeda, who has given his life in this prison in order to introduce the criminal to new life in Christ.'

The Colombian people did, in fact, recognize Oscar for his

labours in the jail. In 1992, the Ministry of Justice named him an official prison chaplain. However, Oscar declined the government salary that came with the appointment, preferring to work as an independent volunteer. Nevertheless, the Justice Ministry's gesture set an important historical precedent. Oscar became the first Protestant pastor selected for a public chaplain post in the history of Colombia, a predominantly Roman Catholic nation.

Oscar finally received the approval of his toughest critic: his own mother-in-law. Mery Perez took years to overcome her anger at God for allowing her daughter to marry an impoverished evangelical – ex-drug addict and street thief, to boot. But she was finally able to forgive the Lord. He also forgave Mery. Today, she regularly attends the Villa Hermosa Evangelical Covenant Church and assists Oscar and Carmenza in their ministry.

'My mum is a Christian today,' Carmenza told a visiting journalist one day in the Osorios' living room. 'It took a long time, about six years. She changed her mind because of the testimony she saw. She has been a witness to the blessings God has given us.

'She is a real dear,' Carmenza added. 'She supports us in every way she can.'

*   *   *

Oscar Osorio quotes three verses near the end of 1 Corinthians 1, to describe the evangelical awakening inside Bellavista: 'But God chose what is foolish in the world to shame the wise, God chose what is weak in the world to shame the strong, God chose what is low and despised in the world, even things that are not, to bring to nothing things that are, so that no human being might boast in the presence of God.'

'Imagine,' he muses, 'the worst persons in the country, criminals like me, who did a lot of damage to our society, we are now the persons God is using to guide it to peace and tranquillity.'

Oscar, Jeannine and other Prison Fellowship volunteers

continue working, not only inside Bellavista but beyond the prison walls to share the gospel of peace. Each weekday morning at 10.30, a local FM radio station broadcasts a half-hour programme live from the Bellavista chapel. The format includes hymns and a brief Bible message. Then, inmates crowd around the microphone to send personal greetings to their families, who regularly tune in to the show.

Prison Fellowship is helping rebuild many of those families. Transformed criminals have been reconciled with estranged wives and abandoned children. Dozens have celebrated weddings in the Bellavista chapel. Mary Luz Correa joined the Prison Fellowship staff upon graduating from the Biblical Seminary to help strengthen these families. Mary Luz sees to it that children get necessary education, that wives find gainful employment and that families who accept Jesus also join a sound, evangelical church.

Mary Luz also works with the 450 inmates in Buen Pastor Women's Prison across town from Bellavista. In order to give the women an opportunity to learn new skills and earn cash during their incarceration, Prison Fellowship opened a seamstress shop in Buen Pastor. Its commercial label is Seditex Ltd. But because Oscar appropriated the sewing machines from a bankrupt clothier, workers have dubbed the operation 'Lazarus Enterprises' – a company 'raised from the dead'.

Upon his graduation from the Biblical Seminary, Lacides Hernandez helped rewrite a handbook used to train prison staff. Lacides designed the new edition using input from Prison Fellowship inmates and ex-offenders. When asked to introduce the training manual to 120 officers-in-training at a Bogotá seminar, Lacides took six interns from the New Life Post Penal Centre along to narrate their life stories. After hearing the testimonies, scores of future prison guards at the workshop accepted Jesus into their own lives.

Today, Bellavista Jail has earned a reputation as the most tranquil prison in Colombia. In 1997, riots exploded in penitentiaries across the country. The mutineers contacted the *caciques* inside Bellavista and demanded they join the uprising.

The Medellín leaders flatly refused. The incident convinced Dr Orlando Lopez that his prison is truly different from the rest.

'The Lord really does have his hand on Bellavista,' Dr Lopez said. 'I say that because every national jail in the country rioted, except for Bellavista. It is at peace because God is in control here.'

Oscar Osorio agrees that the Lord has his hand on Bellavista, but the prison pastor's confidence has not fostered a complacent attitude. 'As far as I'm concerned, we have a big job ahead,' he told a visiting journalist one day in his living room. 'God has given us this ministry in order to spread it to every city in Colombia.'

'We have chaos here in Colombia. People are committing violence, killing. There are prisons in Colombia that right now are living through what Bellavista went through. I believe if the Lord could do this miracle in Bellavista, he can do it in any prison in Colombia and in any part of the world.'

'Bellavista is an open pulpit for the country,' he added. 'It's a place where the country is experiencing the hand of God in one of the world's most dangerous prisons, now transformed.'

*　　*　　*

Oscar Osorio sat across the burnished mahogany desk from Colombia's top lawman, Gustavo De Greiff. The Prosecutor General asked Jeannine Brabon to bring Oscar to his Bogotá office because he had heard of the chaplain's work inside Bellavista and wanted to meet him.

'I have told my staff to back you,' De Greiff told Oscar. 'You're doing what no one else is doing for the country.'

'Tell me, Pastor Osorio,' he added. 'How did you happen to go into prison ministry?'

Oscar recounted the story of his 16-year career as a drug addict and street thief. He described his stints in La Ladera and other jails. He told of hearing the gospel for the first time from Jairo Chalarca and how it changed his life.

'Now, it seems, I am the person God has put in Bellavista to carry the gospel there,' Oscar concluded. 'So, I am content. I'm really very happy.'

The Prosecutor General took another puff on his pipe before he said, 'Very good, Pastor Osorio. The things of God are quite lovely.'

It suddenly occurred to Oscar that he had left out something important.

'Dr De Greiff, there is something very important I ought to tell you,' he said. 'The Bible says in Romans 3.23, "all have sinned and fall short of the glory of God". Sir, I'm afraid if you do not accept Christ into your heart, if you do not repent of your sins, then you will be lost just like any drug addict or *sicario*.'

'I would like to invite you at this moment to ask Jesus to come into your heart,' Oscar added.

The Prosecutor General, dangerous adversary of terrorists and *sicarios*, nemesis of Pablo Escobar, Man of the Year who restored credibility to the Colombian justice system, laid his pipe aside and looked Oscar in the eye. The chaplain returned the steady gaze.

'What do I have to do?' De Greiff asked.

'If you will, sir, repeat a prayer with me right now.'

'Okay,' he said, and got up to close his office door.

When the Prosecutor General had returned to his seat, Oscar rose from his chair and walked around the desk to stand behind him. He took a vial of oil out of his pocket and anointed the hands, feet and forehead of Gustavo De Greiff. Then he began to pray.

Oscar will never forget what happened during that prayer.

'While I was praying with Dr De Greiff, God brought before me an image of my whole life, but in an instant. It was like nothing I have ever experienced, before or since.'

'My whole life passed before my eyes, my childhood, my life in drugs, my crimes, the work in the jail, everything. God brought all of that to my mind. And in that moment, he said to me, "Oscar, all of this was my doing. I did it all."'

Then something happened which was quite out of character

for the veteran prison chaplain. Oscar Osorio, former drug addict who slept on cardboard sheets on the streets of Medellín, ex-offender who met Jesus and returned to jail to preach the gospel, a man God used to bring peace to the Western world's deadliest prison, brushed tears from his eyes.

Epilogue

Bellavista National Jail is not a nice place. Despite the remarkable changes that have taken place there over the past eight years, Bellavista is still an overcrowded, maximum security prison holding thousands of dangerous criminals. Murder and mayhem could flare again, given the right set of circumstances. The staff and volunteers who work inside the prison feel the underlying tension. Visit Bellavista and you will feel it, too. As you leave at the end of the day, you might feel excited to have witnessed history in the making, but you will surely be exhausted for having passed the hours in the presence of danger.

The stress of day-to-day ministry inside Bellavista takes its toll on Prison Fellowship staff. They sometimes differ over strategy, they sometimes experience burn-out, they face the temptation to compromise the high standards of conduct expected of Christian ministers to achieve their goals. Sadly, Oscar Osorio himself succumbed to that temptation. While this manuscript was in the final stages of preparation, word came from Medellín that Prison Fellowship of Antioquia had asked Oscar to resign from the staff because of unethical conduct.

The problems leading to Oscar's dismissal began with Seditex, the seamstress shop established in Buen Pastor women's prison. When Prison Fellowship acquired the sewing machines and industrial equipment from a bankrupt clothier to establish the enterprise, it also assumed nearly $45,000 in debt. Oscar insisted upon personally managing the fledgling business, although he had no training in management. Eventually, Jeannine Brabon and Lacides Hernandez discovered serious financial irregularities involving payments from company clients. Upon further investigation, they found that Oscar had diverted several thousand dollars of Seditex funds, as well as donations to Prison Fellowship, into a private account.

In December 1997, Jeannine, Lacides and arbiters from the faculty of the Biblical Seminary confronted Oscar about the misappropriations. The chaplain admitted his errors and promised to make restitution. He later reneged on that promise. Colleagues then insisted that, as a good-faith demonstration of repentance, Oscar suspend his activities in Bellavista for a period of time. This Oscar refused to do, asserting that Prison Fellowship had no authority to take disciplinary action against him. The board had no option but to dismiss him. 'In accordance with Biblical procedure found in Matthew 18:15–17 and having exhausted all recourse to the end that Oscar recognize his sin and accept restorative discipline, the board has determined to separate him from Prison Fellowship', the written decision reads. 'Nevertheless, our principal objective is his complete restoration.'

At the time of writing, Oscar Osorio continues to direct the New Life Post Penal Centre. It is uncertain what role, if any, he will play in future ministry inside Bellavista. His departure touched off a round of recrimination, threats and even a lawsuit aimed at Prison Fellowship. Nevertheless, the organization will certainly survive this unhappy chapter in its history. In fact, Prison Fellowship of Antioquia seems to be emerging from the crisis in excellent health. In February 1998, a team headed by Lacides Hernandez and Daniel Murillo spent a week in El Bosque District Jail in Barranquilla at the invitation of Major Manuel Ortiz, director of INPEC for Colombia's north coastal region. The visitors held an evangelistic service, the first ever in that facility, according to inmates. Nineteen men, including a prison guard, professed faith in Christ. Major Ortiz approved the team's proposal to construct a building on the prison grounds that will serve as a combination chapel, wood shop and Bible institute. He also invited Prison Fellowship to expand its ministry to every correctional facility in the north coastal region.

Prison Fellowship ministry in Ibague is expanding beyond the formidable walls of the Picaleña Penitentiary as well. In March 1998, Fangio Quiroz reported that inmates transferred out of Picaleña are evangelizing prisoners at Cali, Palmira, Calarca, El Espinal and the Tolima District Jail. The most encouraging sign that the prison ministry remains solid has been the mature reaction to the misappropriation scandal on the part of the church inside Bellavista. Initially confused by the erratic conduct of their chaplain, Christian inmates went to the Bible to sort out the issues of integrity and submission that the crisis raised. After fasting, prayer and frank discussions among themselves, believers announced their endorsement of Prison Fellowship's dismissal of Oscar Osorio and asked him to suspend his visits to the jail.

A veteran preacher was fond of reminding his congregation of a clever dictum: 'In spite of the gates of hell, Christ will build his church . . . and even in spite of us Christians.' Events in Medellín illustrate how true that is. God deserves the glory for what he does in the lives of his creatures, considering what he has to work with. Because of our human failings, no real-life story can ever end with 'and they all lived happily ever after', until we get to heaven, that is.

In the meantime, should you ever have the opportunity to visit Bellavista National Jail, you will be reminded of how broad and long and high and deep the love of Christ is. If God's grace extends to Bellavista, it surely extends to every dark place in the world. If he is able to regenerate the *sicarios* and thieves and terrorists there, he certainly is able to regenerate any one of us.

SPCK

The Society for Promoting Christian Knowledge (SPCK) was founded in 1698. It has as its purpose three main tasks:

- **Communicating the Christian faith in its rich diversity**

- **Helping people to understand the Christian faith and to develop their personal faith**

- **Equipping Christians for mission and ministry**

SPCK Worldwide serves the Church through Christian literature and communication projects in over 100 countries. Special schemes also provide books for those training for ministry in many parts of the developing world. SPCK Worldwide's ministry involves Churches of many traditions. This worldwide service depends upon the generosity of others and all gifts are spent wholly on ministry programmes, without deductions.

SPCK Bookshops support the life of the Christian community by making available a full range of Christian literature and other resources, and by providing support to bookstalls and book agents throughout the UK. SPCK Bookshops' mail order department meets the needs of overseas customers and those unable to have access to local bookshops.

SPCK Publishing produces Christian books and resources, covering a wide range of inspirational, pastoral, practical and academic subjects. Authors are drawn from many different Christian traditions, and publications aim to meet the needs of a wide variety of readers in the UK and throughout the world.

The Society does not necessarily endorse the individual views contained in its publications, but hopes they stimulate readers to think about and further develop their Christian faith.

For further information about the Society, please write to:
SPCK, Holy Trinity Church, Marylebone Road,
London NW1 4DU, United Kingdom.
Telephone: 0171 387 5282